"One of the literary ple
is one of those books
filled to the brim with brilliant writing, with page after page of
hilarious storyline, and equally suffused with sensitivity for
issues of living and dying we all learn to face."

~Grady Harp, Amazon Top 10 Reviewer

"With *In Jupiter's Shadow*, Gregory Gerard shares his
childhood and in doing so, tells a story that vacillates between
heartwarming and heartwrenching. His pop culture references
are funny, poignant, and will resonate with anybody who grew
up in the '70s and/or '80s. A humorous, touching, uplifting
read."

~Georgia Beers, Lammy Award-winning author

"In this disarmingly honest, poignant portrait of innocence
slowly lost, Greg Gerard takes us through the joys and sorrows
of self-discovery, and the importance of emerging from the
shadows of other people's expectations. As a gay "recovering
Catholic," I could relate to the harrowing teenage road paved
with angst, fear, guilt, shame and denial on the journey toward
self-awareness and ultimately self-acceptance. Gerard's gift as
an author is his unpretentious ability to explore deep and
eternal struggles through the lens of youthful optimism and
everyday events, demonstrating the swirling torrents of
confusion and emotion that define all of us in the search for our
selves."

~Greg DiStefano, author of *Breakdown:
Diamonds, Death and Second Chances*

Hiding from others is easy.
Hiding from yourself is trickier.

Growing up in rural Western New York in the late '70s/early '80s, Greg is the youngest of six in a devout Catholic family. They rely on faith to cope with adversity, including a brother's congenital hydrocephalus and the father's alcoholic mood swings. Greg dreams of escape and adventure, mostly through detective stories, which prepares him to tackle the profound mystery he stumbles across—in the bathtub on the second floor.

A fictional detective, Jupiter Jones, provides guidance to explore the clues, but mentorship from a Jesuit priest (an actor with a Hollywood past) ultimately helps Greg reverse his escape path—and solve the mystery between the shadow of "should be" and the light of self-awareness.

www.JupitersShadow.com

In Jupiter's Shadow

Gregory Gerard

INFINITY
PUBLISHING.COM

Copyright © 2009 by Gregory Gerard

ISBN 0-7414-5508-0

Cover design by Gregory Gerard, with thanks for photo enhancement and color feedback from Amy Goodno and Jeff Denmark.

Copy editing by Paul Allison.

Published by:

PUBLISHING.COM

1094 New DeHaven Street, Suite 100
West Conshohocken, PA 19428-2713
Info@buybooksontheweb.com
www.buybooksontheweb.com
Toll-free (877) BUY BOOK
Local Phone (610) 941-9999
Fax (610) 941-9959

Printed in the United States of America
Published September 2009

This story is dedicated to my brother, Paul, who's been "offering it up" since the day he was born.

This story is true, recognizing that memory, at best, is subjective. I have taken some author's liberty with names and details, both to preserve the anonymity of those depicted and make the story more accessible to readers.

Prologue

RUNAWAY PLAN: Cincinnati/Day Sixty-Three (1984)

I grabbed Bufford's keys from the edge of the kitchen counter. Scooping change from my bedroom coin dish into my jeans pocket, I headed down the stairs, two at a time.

I needed to eat.

In the car, I tore out of the Park At Your Own Risk lot. Bufford's tires spat gravel in my wake.

Reaching the grocery store, I headed for the snack aisle. Pulling coins out of my pocket, I counted out five dollars in quarters. I miss Dad's store, I thought, grabbing at a dollar bag of pretzel rods. On my college budget, I could only afford to add a medium-sized bag of M&Ms and a one-liter bottle of 7-UP. It would be enough.

Rushing through the express lane, I hopped into the front seat of my car and yanked at the candy bag. A jagged slit tore down the side as pieces of chocolate flew onto the floor and disappeared down the crack of the seat.

"Shit!" I swore, trying to contain the rest.

I poured the remaining M&Ms into my car's drink tray and opened the pretzel bag more carefully. Positioning it on the seat next to me, I began to chew, watching people come and go.

A man and woman rode up on bicycles. They pulled their bikes together, locking them to a pole in front of the store. Two teenage girls giggled as they walked through a group of parking-lot pigeons. An older couple loaded brown grocery bags into the back seat of a station wagon like Dad's. I could faintly hear them arguing.

Everybody was in pairs. Everybody seemed to know who they were. And how to belong. Everybody except me.

1

I turned the key in Bufford's ignition and tore out of the brightly lit lot. Pigeons scattered in my wake.

Continuing to cram pretzel rods into my mouth, I headed down the one-way street, away from our Park at Your Own Risk apartment.

I had to move. I had to think.

I headed toward the river.

Sheena Easton's Best Kept Secret cassette was still in the stereo. I cranked up the volume and rolled down both front windows.

Streetlights flashed like lightning into the car's interior as I raced through Cincinnati. I pulled onto Route 50, the five-lane highway that hugged the river's bank for miles. I pushed harder on Bufford's accelerator.

The drop-off to the river's edge increased as I left city limits. Sheena's driving beat cut through me. I could feel the bass pounding in my chest, in my belly. I was glad there were hardly any other cars on the road.

Thoughts rushed at me as quickly as the night air that whipped past my head. The speedometer jumped as I worked to outrun them.

Route 50 goes all the way to Ocean City. I could go there.

You don't have enough money for gas, the Jupiter part of my mind whispered.

I thought about the recent conversation with my dad, telling him I wanted to quit college. It conjured the image of him sitting at Big Brick's kitchen table years before, a glass of scotch in his hand, deciding that I, The Caboose, would be the only one of his children to attend Catholic school.

My stomach groaned.

Other images emerged from the rush around me. The shotgun pointed at my chest during the store robbery. My nightly habit in my Big Brick bedroom. Dead flies trapped in the ceiling fixture.

2

Shame and fear flushed fresh and bitter into my throat.

Thoughts of my friend, Roy, surfaced. The raft floating on Duck Lake. Hands flailing *in the burning van.*

Hot tears struggled to flow from the corners of my eyes. I fought them, turning up the radio another notch. I glanced at the mucky water of the Ohio River, but its dark surface reflected only secrets.

Nothing worked. Not quitting college. Not eating my favorite snacks. Not driving eighty miles an hour.

I just couldn't escape.

Part One: Clues

"Any truth is better than indefinite doubt."

~Sherlock Holmes,
The Memoirs of Sherlock Holmes

Cast of Characters

Gregory Gerard: The baby of the family, a.k.a. *The Caboose*; a kid whose interests lie in all things mysterious

Darwin Gerard: Greg's dad; his mellow scotch whiskey persona is known to the family as *Drinking Dar*

Betty Gerard: Greg's mom, dubbed *The Booker*, who won't have fighting in the house

Gram Gerard: Darwin's mom; she tells her grandchildren gritty stories even though Betty doesn't approve

Paul Gerard: Oldest son whose hydrocephalus requires lots of neurosurgery

Molly Gerard: Oldest daughter; Greg's Cincinnati companion and laughing buddy

Kathy Gerard: The thinnest sibling, never seen without a matching outfit

Mike Gerard: A middle child; when he's not taunting Greg, he mentors him

Anne Gerard: The tomboy daughter; her boldness earns Mike's respect

Father McFarland: A parish priest whose confessional inspires obedience

Chapter Zero: Okay (1973)

HALF-WAY THROUGH the homily I started to get anxious.

I was wearing the new pale-gray coat I received on my seventh Christmas. It was toasty inside Saint Patrick's, where the brightly-colored figures on the window glass held the crisp morning outside, yet sent prisms of sunlight to bathe the parishioners in warmth.

Nonetheless, I wore my jacket in the polished wooden pew near the front on the left where we always sat. The coat was my favorite; it had snaps everywhere. I had begun experimenting with the snapping combinations on Christmas morning.

The Gerard clan filled a whole row, like the Dernbecks, who chose the middle right and the McCormicks with their bright red hair, who always came in late and got whatever seat they could.

I sat at the end of the pew, closest to God in His tabernacle, trying to get my arms separated. There were two snaps at the end of each sleeve, designed to make the wrist opening smaller. While Father McFarland spoke passionately about Jesus and His immense love for us, I'd discovered that the right sleeve snaps were a perfect fit to the left and had managed to join all four. Initially pleased with this variation, I now struggled to get my hands free. The game's appeal diminished exponentially with my wrists bound.

My oldest brother, Paul, the church organist, launched into *Faith of Our Fathers* as I lifted both arms and yanked. The snaps didn't yield – but I toppled sideways out of the pew and crashed hard into the center aisle. Hitting the floor with a tremendous *thunk*, I didn't move for a moment, adjusting to my new perspective.

I saw mortified faces as my oldest sister, Molly, jumped to help. I watched Father McFarland, his long beige robe billowing, as he stepped down from the altar to assist.

In the brief moments before they rescued me and I sat safely back in the pew, I lay there struggling, awash in embarrassment and shame, knowing that the priest and my family and the congregation and God were all watching me, wondering if I was okay.

Chapter One: The Plan (1974)

I WAS VISITING Gram the day I hatched my runaway plan. At eight, the youngest in our crowded Western New York farmhouse – Big Brick – I was different from the rest of them; I sensed it.

Everybody else seemed meant to be born, but I'd overheard that I was "a surprise." Everybody else had a regular name, but I went by nicknames: *The Caboose* to my dad; *The Baby* to my mom; *Greg-ums* to the others. Everybody else had a little brother, someone to babysit, boss, or tease. Everybody except me.

I longed to get away through the craggy forest behind our property and discover my own adventure. Something like Nancy Drew or the Hardy Boys might encounter. A place to keep my own secrets.

My grandmother's living quarters had originally been a two-car garage attached to our laundry room. Before she moved in, Dad and some workers converted the space into a one-bedroom suite with a kitchenette and separate entrance. A bay window in the dining area looked out over the three-tiered lawn. Beyond, an expansive field ended in a grove of fruit trees down by the creek.

Gram was not satisfied.

Dad gave her the initial tour because she was his mom. I tagged along.

She looked at the new appliances and fresh paint, her old-lady golden wig and large white earrings dipping forward in silent evaluation. As he showcased the living room, bedroom, kitchen, and bath, I watched her bracelets slide back and forth loosely on her bony wrists.

When they had seen the entire apartment, she drew back, clasped her hands, and nodded toward the tan walls of the living area. "Now, if ya had it to do over again, would ya have picked that same color?"

I held my breath and watched my father closely, to see if he'd yell. A heavyset man, he could raise his powerful voice to shout or swear at a moment's notice.

Instead of shouting, he only snapped "Aw, Mom," and brought the tour to a quick finish. I breathed more easily when he left me and Gram, and returned to our end of the house.

"They put me in the garage," Gram told me later, her muted tangerine dress gathered about her legs as she sat in the living room. I knew she meant my mom and dad, but it was hard to understand why she didn't like the place. I had to share a bedroom with my brother, Mike. With five older siblings, somebody was always telling me what to do. To me, her three rooms seemed spacious and private, a place where she could do *what* she wanted *when* she wanted.

I visited her often, after school or during summer days, winding down the back hallway of our home, through the laundry room, to the double doors that entered her apartment. She served me maple walnut ice cream when we sat at her small Formica table in front of the bay window. She told true crime stories my mother didn't approve of, stories of life ending mysteriously for unlucky victims she'd encountered in her eighty years. Kids, dads, drunks – no one escaped the cool hand of death in her tales.

"He was never up to no good," she shared one day, about a man she'd known a long time ago. "He was a hard man. A drinkin' man. That night he wandered out on the tracks, he'd been drinkin', don't you doubt it." She stared at me over her gray-framed glasses and stabbed an index finger at my face. "That train came along and *good night shirt*!"

I recognized one of the strange phrases that often accompanied her stories. Phrases like *"Get off my foot!"* Or, when she balled her gangly hand into a fist and shook it at someone, *"Smella that, Brother."*

My mind spun. A train clacking through the night. The guy – maybe a crook! – crushed like a soda can, right here in our little town. I sat riveted to the chair, soaking up the intrigue between mouthfuls of creamy maple.

I hadn't been planning to run away. The idea just sprouted one day as I looked out Gram's bay window at the two hundred acres of farmland beyond the barn. Logistics immediately pushed their way through the folds of my mind: what mysteries I might encounter (*find a lost treasure*); which direction I would head (*north*); what gear I might need (*a compass*).

Gram interrupted my thoughts of escape. "Go into the bedroom and get me the picture with five boys in it," she instructed. "They took that picture and a week later one of 'em drowned. *Good night shirt!*"

I located the small frame on top of her sewing table. Reaching for it, I noticed the bottom drawer was not completely shut. A hint of Reese's orange peeked out at me. I opened the drawer another inch, slowly, so it wouldn't squeak. There, snuggled against her stationery and envelopes, lay a ten-pack of peanut butter cups. Perfect sustenance for my trip. I looked around the room. The window was open a crack.

I could do it.

As I slid the drawer fully open, my mind saw Father McFarland pull back the tiny window in the confessional at our church, Saint Patrick's. There in the darkness, I would have to shamefully whisper of my theft, praying the mesh screen masked my identity. He'd whisper back my penance, concern evident in his low tones. *Would it be ten Hail Marys? Apologize to my grandmother? Something worse?*

I loved most things about church. Mystery peeked out at me from every corner; darkened shadows whispered the secrets of Saints long dead. At Mass, I watched the priest lift his shrouded arms toward Heaven, muttering prayers only God could hear. Desire to be holy like him, like my mother, always flooded me. To be a son of God. To belong.

But the confessional was another story. Whenever I entered the tiny wooden room, I felt embarrassed and exposed. My budding crime came to an abrupt halt. I considered the Reese's carefully. *Was it worth it?*

"Do ya see it, Honey?" Gram called from the living room.

"Yeah, I got it."

I grabbed the frame and, with no time to consider further consequences, the candy as well. I shoved the ten-pack through the narrow gap of the open window. The orange wrapper flashed as it fell to the grass outside.

I handed Gram the frame. She pointed to the different children in the aged photo, including the one who had met with an untimely death. Normally this would hold my attention, but I worried about the peanut butter cups melting in the afternoon sun.

She talked mother's tears; I pictured tears of chocolate dripping off my candy. I finally told her I had to go and raced through the laundry room to one of Big Brick's back doors. Outside, I crawled low under her window to snatch the Reese's. I felt them through the wrapper. They were intact.

I brought the orange package to my bedroom and laid it on my sleeping bag, then gathered more supplies. A pillow, some Hardy Boy books. I looked at the pack and evaluated. It needed a goodbye note.

I sat on the corner of my bed and wrote a long letter to my family, listing how sorry I was to leave, but for them not to miss me. I drew eight round faces – my mom, dad, gram, my five older siblings – and penned streams of tears running down their tiny paper cheeks. There wasn't a dry eye on the page.

The goodbye note went in with the other supplies. I rolled the sleeping bag into a tight cylinder and hid it in the back of my closet.

The excitement of my impending departure distracted me from the guilt of my theft. I did worry that Gram would miss the candy and tell my dad but, as two days passed, the paternal wrath I anticipated never materialized. I continued to imagine my adventure, waiting for the right opportunity to escape.

The next morning I woke to rain, a steady, pounding curtain of water on the upstairs windows. Using the delay of weather to tighten my plan, I decided to add a map to my runaway kit. On my adventure, I'd travel further than our rural twin towns, Palmyra and Macedon, known as Pal-Mac to the locals, where I'd lived all my life. Heading to the downstairs bookshelves, I pulled out a thin road atlas – which promised *Up-To-Date Construction Information* in a little yellow bubble – and carried it upstairs.

Opening my bedroom door, I discovered Mike and Anne, my brother and sister, sitting in the center of the carpet.

Mike was six years my senior and wiser about everything. He wore his brown hair short and straight-cut across the bangs, giving him a serious, tough-guy edge. He wrestled at school – which showed in the tight bulge of his arm muscles.

Just a year younger than Mike, Anne was often at his side. My tomboy sister, her hair hung in a long dark splash to her shoulders, curling slightly near the ends, as if in defiance to the straightness of the rest. Her boldness earned my brother's respect. I envied her.

My sleeping bag lay between them on the floor, unrolled. Mike had my goodbye note in his hand and was reading it aloud.

They were in hysterics.

"*What – is – your – problem*?" he asked, barely able to get the words out.

I reached for the note, my face flushing with familiar warmth. He held it toward me, waving it back and forth. I grabbed, missed, then snatched it from him. I tore it up quickly.

"So you're gonna run away?" Anne transitioned from laughter to concern.

My meticulous plan evaporated into embarrassment.

"NO," I said.

The impact was gone – now that they knew about it. Besides, it was *really* raining outside, and the reality of sleeping on soggy grass diluted the portrait of my grand escape.

"Where'd you get the peanut butter cups?" Anne interrupted my thoughts.

"At the store," I said, mentally adding *lying* to the list I'd review with Father McFarland, as Mike tore open the package and divided the spoils among us.

RUNAWAY PLAN: Cincinnati/Day One (1984)

My sister, Molly, and I arrived in Cincinnati, my college destination, nine hours after pulling out of Big Brick's driveway. I welcomed the chance to get away from the turmoil that tightened my insides.

The downtown skyline was brightly lit. A huge suspension bridge stretched out across the Ohio River, connecting Cincinnati to Kentucky. The dark, slow water drew my attention.

I'd read about the river back at high school. One of the deepest waterways in the country, it rumbled through Ohio on its way to the Mississippi. I wondered how many secrets had been swallowed up in its murky depths.

I turned my attention to the lighted skyline. My sister had described the city to me in letters and over the phone. In person, the buildings loomed much taller than anything we had back in Rochester.

"Holy crap," I said.

"Pretty cool, huh?" Molly said. "I love living in a big city."

She gave street directions to the apartment she'd picked out for us at the beginning of the summer. The closer we got, the more trash I saw scattered along the curbs.

A few people loitered in front of a massive brick apartment building. Carved stone trim framed the many windows, but it was crumbled and cracked, like some of the surrounding bricks.

"Welcome home." Molly pointed. "Turn right in here!"

"Just ignore the Park at Your Own Risk sign," she continued as we entered the lot. "I've been here for months and there haven't been any problems."

Was she serious? We'd never had a sign like that back in Pal-Mac. I parked and looked around. The beat-up, rusty cars with their Ohio license plates made my car, Bufford, a '77 Plymouth Fury, look out of place and unwelcome. I knew how he felt.

I glanced at all my belongings in the back seat and groaned. My sister had prepared me for the long haul up four flights. The elevator hadn't worked since she moved in.

Molly got out and we surveyed the pile together. "Okay, let's just take up the stuff we really need right now and leave the rest for later," she suggested.

I reached in and selected my Sheena cassettes, the Xavier University orientation packet, and my suitcase. Molly grabbed the nearest box, stuffed with clothes.

Before locking the car, I draped a couple of tee shirts across the rest of the load in the back seat. I tried to arrange them as though I had thrown them there by accident. Jupiter Jones, my favorite detective, would have taken more elaborate precautions to thwart potential crooks, but I made do.

"Just in case," I said.

We climbed two lengthy flights, then stopped, gasping for breath. As the two heaviest Gerard children, we looked at each other and began to laugh at our lack of fitness. "I guess nobody's gonna mistake me for Mary Lou Retton," Molly joked. Our laughter increased, making the next two flights even more difficult.

At the top, Molly unlocked a plain wooden door and both of us plopped down at her kitchen table.

"This – is – the – kitchen," she gasped out, waving her hand around. I detected a faint turpentine smell.

"Have you – been painting?" My lungs began to fill normally ·again. She stood and, opening the cupboard above the sink, pulled out a small jar. Several paint-brush handles stuck out. The smell intensified.

"Yeah, I painted the kitchen in June and I was soaking the brushes. I sorta forgot about 'em." The giggles returned, a hot, anxious release after the long day on the road – and, for me, the meaning behind the trip.

I walked to the first room down the hall, my bedroom. The twelve-foot ceiling soared above a mammoth fireplace encased in marble. A beat-up brown couch sat facing the marble. Molly pointed to it.

"I pulled the couch outta the trash last week. I thought you might want it. Danny helped me carry it up. He's our upstairs neighbor. You can meet him later." I sat, sinking deep into the couch until only my legs and torso were visible.

"So what's it feel like to be in your first apartment?" she asked, sinking a comparable depth into the opposite end.

"It's pretty awesome," I said, surveying the space. "Show me the rest of the place." We struggled to eject ourselves from the couch.

More laughter.

In the next room, clothes were strewn everywhere, an ironing board standing sentinel above them. "I always wanted to have a big enough place to set up the iron and not have to take it down," Molly said, walking further to a small bend in the hall. "When I got to this point, I knew this was the place!"

Beyond the bend, the apartment stretched on for another thirty feet, ending in floor-to-ceiling windows.

"Holy crap!" I said for the second time that day.

"Bathroom, living room, my bedroom," she checked them off with her fingers as we continued the tour. "You can tell it used to be a pretty ritzy apartment building, but since the neighborhood has gone down a bit, it's spacey – and in my price range."

I looked out one of the tall windows. A couple of guys dressed in ripped jeans and dirty tee shirts sat on the curb far below. I thought of the robberies at our father's store. "Do you feel safe here?"

"Yeah, it's been fine. The landlord and his wife live right next door and Danny lives upstairs, so I feel safe. I just love that it's so big! We can co-egg-zist but each have our own space."

I caught my sister's enthusiasm and we made dinner plans to celebrate our new place. I welcomed the distraction from the thoughts that choked my introspective moments.

Thoughts about Roy's death.

Thoughts about my own damnation.

Chapter Two: Prickers and Fudge (1974 continued)

AS AN ALTERNATIVE to running away, I spent the next month making mini-treks through the two hundred acres behind Big Brick. My dog, Pete, our collie-beagle puppy, accompanied me on every trip. I loved the solitude of the outdoors – a contrast to our active household.

We were eight in total – Mom, Dad, and six kids. Nine, if you counted Gram. "We're like The Brady Bunch," I once pointed out to my brother, Mike. "Except our *order* is wrong, boy, girl, *girl*, boy, girl, boy," I compared us to my ideal TV family, seeking a pattern, as was my habit. "Paul, Molly, *Kathy*, Mike, Anne. And then me – I'm the *last* Gerard."

"The Brady Bunch are queers," Mike snapped.

Our property fostered nature in every direction: a pear tree with a hollow center near the creek; cattails and field grass circling the pond; a tangled patch of shoulder-high thistles behind the garage. The latter confounded my father. He and Mom wanted a swimming pool in place of the prickly weeds.

My dad attacked the area with vigor, using the bulldozer he'd purchased to assist with ongoing renovations at Big Brick. His balding head gleamed as he dozed the thistles to the ground, spreading the displaced earth in even layers across the bumpy acres behind Big Brick. One of the guys who'd helped build Gram's apartment rode a small tractor behind him and spread grass seed.

Four weeks later, Dad exploded with rage when he discovered that the thistles, bulldozed into apparent oblivion, had seeded with the new grass. Spiky fronds pushed up everywhere among the fuzzy clumps of green. Two acres of prickers. I watched from the safety of the garage as my father kicked at the unfriendly weeds with his heavy work shoes. Pete hung at my side, whining softly.

Dad launched into one of his rants, yelling about Murphy's Law, his face twisted into a fierce scowl. After a few minutes, he headed in my direction. I pretended to be organizing our croquet set as he entered the garage.

I wondered why Dad got so angry so often. *Was he mad because Gram acted like he never did anything right?* Mom had told me a few things about my father's childhood. That his own dad had left town when he was twelve, right after the divorce. How it was just him and Gram during the Depression. How he'd played piano in the local bar when he was fourteen. When he'd started drinking.

He'd flown a bomber in World War II, but he rarely talked about that. Mostly, when he wasn't yelling, he sat at the dining room table in the evenings, drinking scotch whiskey and writing long letters to his relatives in California – the great aunts and uncles I had never met. He never yelled when he drank. Instead, he became a mellow talker, using big, formal phrases like "*considering your command of the English language*" and "*I'll accept that course of action.*"

We called this version of my father *Drinking Dar*, a shortcut of his first name, Darwin, to reflect the change in his personality. After just one glass of whiskey, his vocabulary trebled and smooth words flowed from his mouth – although he often didn't remember what we had talked about the next day. Drinking Dar never made my stomach feel tight.

Entering the garage, my father scrounged through the piles of lawn equipment and pulled out a wooden pole with a metal fork at one end. Dad turned toward me. I noticed his scowl had softened, as it always did after one of his rants.

"I got a job for you, Caboose. I'll pay you a penny for each pricker you pick." He led me outside and demonstrated. "Just stick the business end into the ground like this." In response to his

20

quick jab, a thistle popped from the ground like the head of a dandelion flicked off by a thumbnail. "You have to get the root or it'll just grow back." He looked at me. "You have any questions before I run some errands?" I shook my head.

My father handed me the tool and climbed into his station wagon. I watched him pull out of the winding drive and felt a guilty sense of relief that often accompanied his exits.

I thrust the metal groove into the ground and began my tally. *A penny a pricker.* The sun intensified as I worked; the day was a scorcher. I spotted Gram in her bay window. We both waved. *Maybe she knows a story about somebody who was stabbed to death with a pricker-picker*, I thought. *Good night shirt.*

An hour later, I reached my first hundred. *A dollar.* I leaned on the tool, feeling a chapping in my palms from the rough wooden handle. Pete had retired to the cool shade of the garage.

Mom stuck her head out of Big Brick's back door and called for me to come inside. "See ya later, boy," I waved to Pete. More wagging.

Our house was quieter than usual today. Molly, who'd just enrolled in nursing school, had gone to the mall to buy a uniform. Kathy, my sister who refused to be seen without a matching outfit, went along for the shopping opportunity. Mike and Anne had left hours earlier, riding their bikes toward town. And Paul, the organist at Saint Patrick's, was playing a wedding.

"How's it going?" my mother asked when I came into the kitchen.

"Good – I picked one hundred so far!"

"Good for you, Honey."

"My hands are a little sore," I said, holding them out in front of me.

"You should probably wear some gloves. But you go ahead and take a break for now. You're not going to get them all in one day." She looked down at me. "I'm going to make some fudge and I thought you'd like to help."

"You bet!" I shouted. Mom smiled at my enthusiasm. In our family, making fudge was a ritual almost as sacred as attending Mass.

"Wash your hands," she instructed.

Dousing my hands in the sink's soapy water, I rinsed quickly, then pulled a chair toward our countertop range. I watched my mother closely. Her ample day dress fluttered as she turned from the stove to reach into the cupboard. Her brown hair was shorter than any of my sisters, but it had the same Gerard thickness. Hints of gray peeked out from all over her head.

Mom matched my father in girth, but never in temperament. Instead, she often laughed and sang. "Sing with me," she coaxed as she pulled sugar and vanilla down from the cupboard. We launched into the family favorites, including *You Wore a Tulip* and *Good Night, Ladies*.

My mother heaped cocoa and butter into the fudge pan. I studied the swirl patters while she stirred the batter. Our red-and-white checkered pot holder lay on the counter nearby. My finger flicked the burn mark on its corner, a reminder of the time Dad had been drinking and had caught the pot holder on fire.

It had been a hasty accident – a quick flame, a quick douse under the faucet – but, like the blackened edge of the pot holder, its effects had lingered. Now whenever my father pulled out the whiskey bottle and puttered around the stove, I saw my mother keep an extra eye on him.

When the fudge mixture bubbled to the correct rhythm, Mom poured the gooey mass onto a platter and handed me the nearly empty pan. She gathered the other utensils and turned to the sink. "Good cooks clean up as they go," she instructed.

I worked at the fudge pan with a spoon for awhile, scooping out every trace of chocolate. Surrendering it for washing, my focus turned to the fudge platter. I stared at the shiny blob, willing it to solidify. "Did you eat fudge when you were a kid?" I asked her.

She looked over from the sink where she was elbow-deep in sudsy water.

"Yes, Honey. It was the Depression when I was little, so nobody had any money. But we always had the supplies for fudge. We'd make a batch every Friday night.

"We had to make a lot of sacrifices back then, but Dad was a salesman and Mum – that's your Gramma Trudy; you never knew her – she was a nurse, so we were luckier than some people. Dad and Mum always found work.

"There were six of us kids and I slept on a little square blanket on the floor of my brother John's room." She stopped lifting the dishes out of the sink and stared out the window. The afternoon sun lit her dark hair with a soft glow, like the halo around the Blessed Mother's statue at Saint Patrick's.

She looked at me and smiled. "Enjoy yourself, Kiddo. It goes so fast," she said, taking a seat and slicing the fudge into chunks.

When we'd each had a couple of pieces and all the dishes were cleaned and dried, I headed into the adjoining family room. My favorite cartoon, *The Flintstones*, was just beginning. I flicked on the TV while Mom pulled out her car keys. "Greg, I've got to run some errands. Gram is back in her apartment if you need anything. And the other kids should be home pretty soon. Okay?"

"Okay," I said, barely glancing up from the television. Mom kissed my head and left.

Fifteen minutes into *The Flintstones*, I heard Big Brick's front door bash open against its frame as it sometimes did when the east wind picked up.

"Goddamn it!" I heard my father yell.

My gut seized.

There was a clattering crash as though someone had dumped a load of cans onto the slate floor of the foyer. The family room door, a thick slab of solid oak, burst open. It swung rapidly on its antique cast-iron hinges, the doorknob striking the wall just below the family crucifix. Jesus' body gave a little jerk as the door rebounded.

Dad entered, his face twisted tight, his bushy eyebrows jutting toward me. "What're you doing?" he growled. He clutched an empty grocery sack in his right hand. The bottom was ripped wide open.

"Watching Flintstones," I said.

"Well, get outside! I told you to work on those prickers!" He slapped at the TV's power switch. The image of Fred and Barney blinked out, leaving a small dot in the center of the screen.

My father came at me. I jumped out of my mom's rocker, my stomach completing the square knot it had begun with the crash of the front door.

He grabbed my arm and yanked me toward the back hall. "March!" he commanded, wrenching the back door wide. Thrusting me through, he kicked at me, landing a quick smack on my bottom, then slammed the door shut behind me.

I didn't fall, but my rear end burned with the sting of his shoe. I stood for a moment, blinking at the brilliant afternoon. Tears welled in my eyes.

Pete appeared from the open garage doorway and greeted me enthusiastically. His sandpaper tongue dragged across my face, helping my stomach to settle.

Reconsidering my runaway plan, I returned to the prickers. Two hours passed before my mother pulled into the driveway and I felt safe enough to go back inside our house.

RUNAWAY PLAN: Cincinnati/Day Two (1984)

The next morning, Molly led me upstairs and knocked on the door of the apartment directly above us. A young blond man answered. A bounding German shepherd pushed past him into the hall. "Danny, I want you to meet my brother, Greg," she said.

"Hi Greg!" he shook my hand. I drank in his blue eyes, his sweet smile, his worn jeans. Could he be gay? I wasn't sure how to tell. Jupiter Jones had never taught me that deductive skill.

"Hi," I returned his handshake, trying not to stare.

"And this is Chauncey," Molly said as the dog jumped at me, demanding my attention. I got to my knees and tried to greet Danny's energetic pet.

"Hi Chauncey!" I said. He heard his name and landed on me, his tongue drenching my face. I thought of my own dog, Pete, and our twilight walks back at home. The memory tugged at my heart, but I fought it. I was done with home; this was college; this was my escape.

I had eight days before classes began, but I wanted to scope out the Xavier campus. Like any good detective.

Telling my sister I'd catch up with her later, I popped Sheena's Best Kept Secret cassette into Bufford's player and headed to Xavier University. I sang along enthusiastically with my favorite songs – Telefone, Almost Over You, Let Sleeping Dogs Lie.

I neared my new school. A plush carpet of grass surrounded the entire campus. At the center, a brick castle-like string of buildings towered above a long, sloping hill. It was much bigger than McQuaid, my Jesuit high school back home.

From inside the car, I mentally ticked off the locations I'd seen on my orientation map. Football field. Student parking. Chapel. On paper, everything had seemed orderly and close.

In person, it was immense.

On the way home I picked up a five-scoop sundae from a Cincinnati ice cream shop. Alone at the apartment, I devoured the ice cream.

Later, I packed my journal, beach towel, and Sheena cassettes into my book bag. I climbed two more flights up the stairwell, walkman in hand, and headed to the roof.

Molly had done some sunbathing up there. She told me the roof was available to all tenants. I prayed none of them were up there today. I wanted to be alone. I wanted to think.

I cracked open the door at the top of the stairs and stepped out. Silvery tar covered the surface – to reflect the sun, I guessed. It felt hot against my bare feet, but the peaceful stillness immediately overrode the sting. Other than a few pigeons, who skittered away at my approach, I was the only one there.

Our building stood taller than the others in the neighborhood, so I could see for miles in every direction. The downtown skyline and river to the south. The hint of green hills to the north.

The quiet reminded me of the field behind Big Brick's barn. Despite my efforts to move on, a heavy wave of longing washed over me, intensified beyond the levels I'd learned to cope with. The image of the Jesuit castle on the hill flooded my mind.

I spread the towel and lay in the warm sun, wondering what college would be like. And, even if I were careful, whether my secret would be found out.

Chapter Three: Secrets (1974 continued)

MOM CARRIED FORWARD the theme of self-sacrifice from her childhood to our household. If we grumbled about having too much homework or complained about jobs that Dad assigned us around Big Brick, she would gently encourage us to *offer it up*.

As Catholics, we knew that God welcomed our smallest sacrifices: for the conversion of sinners on Earth; for the saving of souls in Purgatory; for the preparation of our own hearts to receive Jesus in Holy Communion. When something was unpleasant and unchangeable, it was to be offered up to Heaven.

I had some personal experience with Catholic sacrifice. The previous spring, I discovered a book on the downstairs bookshelves: *Our Lady of Fatima*. In just a couple of days, I devoured the story of the Blessed Virgin – Jesus' mom – visiting three children in Portugal back in 1917. Each of them had seen Our Lady floating on a cloud while they knelt by a stone. They'd been entrusted with secrets, just like something out of Nancy Drew, except real.

The kids in the book made sacrifices to help the souls of sinners everywhere. They wore wool against their skin and suffered itchy consequences. They slept on boards and didn't complain about being tired. Instead, they *offered it up*.

The story fascinated me. I wanted to do my part, to help the sinners' souls. And maybe, if I tried the same thing, the Blessed Mother would appear and tell *me* secrets.

In the barn, I found a couple of thin boards. I sneaked them into the house when Mike wasn't around and placed them underneath the bottom sheet on my bed. I got to my knees. "God, I promise to sleep on these boards for the conversion of sinners," I whispered.

The wood was stiff and the edges jutted up through the cotton, pressing into my stomach and hip. I repositioned the boards long ways, so my body would fit on a single slab. That was a little better.

I slept restlessly for a few nights. The fourth night, Mom tucked me in. She touched the bed and felt the hardness.

"What's this?" she asked me.

I explained what I was doing.

"Oh no, Honey, that's not necessary, God doesn't expect you to do that."

We removed the boards and she kissed me goodnight. As I lay back on the soft sheets, I reconsidered the whole situation. It seemed that God *did* want the kids in Fatima to make sacrifices like that – and they were only my age. Plus, Mom was the one who taught us to offer things up in the first place.

Nonetheless, she said not to sleep on the boards and, other than Father McFarland, she was the holiest person I knew, so I listened.

If desire for holiness didn't provide enough incentive, Mom had a second line of defense to stave off our grumbling. "Think of what Paul's been through," she'd say. That always brought us to a quick stop. Our oldest brother had problems that eclipsed any complaints we could muster.

I knew Paul had indentations on his skull from brain surgery, but I wasn't clear on the details. One day in our shared bedroom, I asked Mike about it.

Setting down the barbells he'd been assembling, he looked straight at me. "When Paul was six weeks old, his head got really big and his eyes started going from side to side. Mom and Dad rushed him to the hospital and found out he had hydrocephalus. Do you know what that is?"

I'd heard the word around our house. A lot. "Not really." I lay across my bedspread and listened as Mike continued.

"That means your brain doesn't drain fluid the way it's supposed to. It makes your head get really big and it'll kill you if you don't relieve the pressure. He was probably born with it."

His voice lowered. "That's when the miracle happened."

I sat up straight. Miracles were like *mysteries*.

"When Paul was a baby, only three doctors in the whole United States knew how to put in a shunt. That's the tube Paul has inside him to drain fluid off his brain. The miracle is that God had one of those doctors right at Paul's hospital in Rochester."

"Wow!"

"When he was little, he had to go back for a lot of surgeries to get his shunt to work right. It was such a new thing, it would sometimes back up. They had to try different ways to make it work. At one point, they even drilled a little hole in his skull to let the fluid drain off if the pressure got too much. The spot used to swell up like a ping pong ball whenever he got a headache and he'd just pump it up and down. Whatever was clogging his shunt would clear out and the lump would go down."

"Is that why he's got a dent on the top of his head?"

"Yeah, that's where the hole is." Mike picked up the barbells and continued their assembly. I sensed the end of the story.

My brother looked at me as I stood. He paused, then spoke. "That's why Mom's so protective of him, you know," he added. "When he has headaches or throws up, she gets worried that he might have to go back to the hospital. And she'd *always* afraid that he might hurt his head by lifting heavy stuff or tripping and falling." I nodded in understanding. I'd seen our mother fuss over Paul many times.

???

A month after my father kicked me out the back door, our backyard was pricker-free – thanks to a chemical weed treatment by the local garden store. Dad had finally called them after I'd picked twenty-three dollars worth with no discernable progress.

Lush grass now circled Big Brick, the newly installed pool, and our willow and maple trees, stretching long and green toward the barn. At our lawn's borders, overgrown fields extended in every direction. Beyond that, stalks of corn sloped in gentle rows past the pond up to the edge of the forest. A farmer from down the road owned the cornfield; he spent every spring tilling and planting with his tractor.

Together, Pete and I spent July searching the entire property for crooks or buried treasure. Things like the Hardy Boys always found. So far, the only evidence I'd discovered was three lonely boards – a makeshift ladder – nailed to a huge maple tree at the forest's edge. Maybe kids had once built a tree house there. *Or maybe thieves had used the tree for a lookout. Back before I was born.*

Throughout our investigation, no other mysteries surfaced, which is why my brother's bet took me off guard. Mike bet me twenty dollars that there was a secret room somewhere inside our barn.

I considered his proposition carefully. I only had twenty-three dollars – my pricker funds – in my account at the Macedon branch of the Rochester Savings Bank. I'd worked too hard for this money to part with such a significant chunk unnecessarily.

Experience had taught me to be cautious around my brother. At eight years old to his fourteen, I often worked to convince him I was a capable sidekick, like Joe Hardy was to Frank. Circumstances had encouraged the opposite.

When he'd insisted I ride shotgun on the snowmobile the previous winter, I cried, convinced I'd fly off during one of his speedy turns. When we'd cleaned the cellar that spring, I ran from a spider, even after he'd yelled at me to be brave.

Betting ground seemed safer territory, especially considering the detecting Pete and I had accomplished. Granted, twenty dollars was a *lot* of money, but I wouldn't lose any limbs or be poisoned by some vengeful tarantula.

I accepted his challenge.

We headed outside and approached the barn's main entrance. My brother slid back one of the massive wooden doors as daylight showered the interior.

The barn had once been used for dairy production, but only hints of the former occupants remained. A rusted neck clamp. The smell of petrified dung. Now our family used the space to store

30

extra belongings. Mike and I stepped around boxes of Dad's tools, Gram's spare furniture, and Mom's record albums. We climbed a ladder to the next level.

Most of the second floor was wide open – like the insides of an armored dinosaur. The frame of the tin ceiling was visible; no drywall covered the guts. Very little natural light permeated the darkness, with only two small windows at either end, fifty feet above our heads. Twin ceiling bulbs fought unsuccessfully to illuminate what the windows couldn't.

Pigeons had roosted in the rafters over the years. They rustled nervously at our entrance. Mike stopped and gave a loud "HEY!" which reverberated in the cavernous space. The satisfying sound of flapping rose in a crescendo as the birds relocated to the south end of the barn. Darkness masked their flight.

I turned to face my brother. "Okay, where's this secret room?" I said, trying to sound like a tough negotiator. In response, my brother led me to the raised platform at the north end of the second floor. We called this area "the stage."

I'd never had the nerve to venture onto the stage's surface. Instead of nailed-down flooring like the rest of the upstairs, the stage looked hastily assembled. Long planks lay loose across the stage's support beams. Bare holes between the planks showed light from the first floor – holes big enough to stuff a kid's body through. Through them, I could see the first floor fifteen feet below. Enough of a drop to make my skull as lumpy as Paul's.

The stairway to the stage consisted of three short boards nailed to a rickety wooden frame. I tested the first. It creaked under my weight. "I'm not sure about this," my voice cracked as my Hardy Boy resolve diminished.

Mike worked his way across the stage. I made it to the second, then third stair, imagining how my head would look cracked apart on the cement below, goo flowing freely from the gash. Gram would retell the story for years to come. "*Good night shirt!*" would become my epitaph.

"Come on!" Mike pressured me. "It's safe. I've been up here before. You just have to stay over the supports." He stepped

31

carefully, always keeping his weight directly above one of the massive support beams. I watched as he reached his goal: a half-wall on the far side of the stage, which hid the area beyond.

"See?" he said, reaching a wooden ladder on the far wall. He looked back at me and lost his patience. "Greg, why are you so scared all the time?! I wouldn't tell you to do it if it wasn't okay!" He turned away and started up the rungs.

Weighing the humiliation of my brother's disappointment against the image of my brains splattered on concrete, I gingerly stepped onto the planks. I advanced in small, precise steps, ensuring I didn't come close to any of the gaping holes. My stomach remained a tight knot across the short distance. Reaching the far side, I hugged the built-in ladder in relief.

"Come on up!" Mike said. "We're almost there."

Securely fastened ladders seemed less frightening in comparison. I climbed to the top of the half-wall and discovered a twin ladder on the opposite side. It led down into darkness. My brother had already climbed to the bottom and had flicked on the flashlight he'd brought. With the stage crossing behind me, the intrigue of a secret room quelled the panic in my gut.

I crawled down the ladder into the deep wooden well, holding tightly to each rung. Reaching my foot out, I tested the floor. Dirt covered the bottom like a rug; I had to push it around with my shoe to find the solid boards beneath. A swirl of dust shot into the flashlight beam as a sneezing fit seized me.

My brother laughed at me. "You gonna make it?"

"Yeah," I said, holding my nose to stave off more sneezes.

My curiosity overrode the threat of insects lurking in the pitch-black space. It was as good as any hidden room I'd ever read about in a mystery story! In our current location, we couldn't be seen from any point inside or outside of the barn. If we stayed absolutely quiet, nobody could hear us. Crooks on my tail might search for hours in vain.

We walked around, dust rising in a thick cloud from our movements. I kept a clamp-hold on my nose as Mike measured the distance across the space with his stride. "I'd say it's about twelve feet by twelve feet. Pretty good, huh? Whattya think?"

"It's great!" I said. "How did it get here?"

"These were grain bins back when this was a cow barn. There's three of them total, but this is the biggest one. It makes a pretty good secret room, huh?" I nodded and sneezed at the same time.

My brother laughed again. "Well, you lose the bet," he reminded me. "I know you only have twenty-three dollars in the whole world, so *I guess* you don't have to pay me."

I smiled to myself. Frank Hardy often looked out for Joe's best interests. Once in awhile, Mike did the same for me.

"It's great!" I said again, imagining the bin filled with grain. Maybe a farmhand had once fallen in. Maybe he'd suffocated. My neck hair bristled appreciatively.

The dust began to settle as we stopped our exploring. Mike held the flashlight beneath his chin, casting a fierce shadow across his features. "Greg Gerard is a boy retard," he moaned in a raspy voice.

I punched his muscled arm. "You know Mom said not to say 'retard'!" Mom *never* let us use that word. Especially around Paul.

Mike shined the flashlight into my eyes as if in defiance of Mom's authority, then resumed the below-the-chin position. "Wanna know another secret?" he whispered.

"Okay," I said.

My brother leaned closer. "Do you know how a mom and a dad make a baby?" he asked.

I stared at him, searching for a clue, but his expression remained superior and indifferent. From his tone, I suspected this secret was something naughtier than a hidden room in the barn.

I turned the clues over in my mind. Married people had babies. Didn't it just happen after you got married? I imagined my parents trying to make a baby. I knew they slept in the same bed. I'd seen them both in the bathroom once with no clothes on, getting ready to go out to dinner. Maybe – hmmm. I envisioned my mom and dad standing naked, rubbing their bottoms together, cooking up another kid.

I shook my head.

He shrugged his shoulders. "Maybe I shouldn't tell you. After all...you are only eight."

"Come on!" I yelled, louder than was allowed indoors. Whenever our voices rose in volume inside Big Brick, Mom reminded us of her main rule: "I won't have fighting in this house!" Here in the barn, we were safe to be as loud as we wanted.

"Well...I *guess* it's okay..." he offered one final tease, then began to explain how it all worked. Penises and vaginas. Sperm and egg. My eyes widened. It sounded silly – and bizarre.

"You're making this up!" I said.

"Greg, I am not!" Athough I didn't always agree with my brother, I could sense when he was lying. This was the truth.

I relented, trying to imagine a girl touching me *down there*. My stomach grumbled.

"That's gross," I said out loud. Mike laughed.

We climbed out of the secret room and made our way slowly back across the stage. I continued to offer passionate objections to what he'd told me. My brother laughed again. "You'll understand about making babies when you get older," he assured me. "You'll *want* to do it."

I deferred to his older wisdom but, listening to the anxious rustling of the pigeons far above our heads, I wondered.

Part Two: On The Case

*"One should always look for a possible alternative,
and provide against it.
It is the first rule of criminal investigation."*

~Sherlock Holmes,
The Return of Sherlock Holmes

Cast of Characters

Caroline: Greg's new neighbor; her parents' sex book is hidden in the guest room drawer

Sister Helen: Her guitar playing brings Greg closer to his favorite movie, *The Sound of Music*

Adam: Greg's grammar-school best friend who can't resist the game of Truth or Dare

Father Fredricks: A dour priest whose lesson on masturbation leaves little room for pleasure

Father Deckman: His friendly laugh charms parishioners

Jupiter Jones: The brainy, overweight kid detective in The Three Investigators mystery series; Greg emulates him at every opportunity

Merk: An opinionated bus driver and self-proclaimed karate expert

Gaila: A first date for Greg; the afternoon begins with popcorn and ends with vomit

Father Jameson: A religion teacher whose eyebrows convey the sin of Sodom

John: Greg's high school buddy who just can't make it to class on time

Chapter Four: The Nature of Sexuality (1977)

"NOTHING SOUNDS HOLLOW," I said to Caroline, my newest friend. She glanced up at me from the floor, where she'd been crawling around examining the knotty pine baseboards.

Caroline and her parents had moved into the cobblestone house across the street from Big Brick several months earlier. In contrast to our full-figured family, they were all bone-thin. A small bowl of brown hair, almost blonde, cupped Caroline's head. Although she was three years younger than I, we'd discovered a mutual interest in Nancy Drew mysteries and had quickly become friends.

Just like Big Brick, her house was built in the 1840s. At school, while studying the Civil War, I'd learned that our towns, Macedon and Palmyra, were active in the Underground Railroad. The teacher assured us it wasn't something actually beneath the soil – that "Underground Railroad" meant slaves traveled through our towns from the South to freedom in Canada.

Regardless, I couldn't help wondering if someone just might have constructed a complex network of tunnels to help the travelers along their journey. It could be Western New York's biggest secret.

Caroline and I adopted the mission to search our houses for defunct passageways. Finding a hidden tunnel – a cobweb-ridden staircase, a squirreled-away map – would almost be like solving a mystery.

Her parents had worked to keep the look and feel of nineteenth century America, preserving original woodwork and window glass, filling their house with antique furniture and lace coverlets. In the museum-like atmosphere, a secret passageway seemed within our grasp.

Today we concentrated on their guest room. In response to my report about hollow walls, Caroline nodded, stood, and brushed off her corduroys. She shut the door and set the latch into its notch. "You wanna see something?" she asked.

"Sure," I said, my investigative senses on full alert.

Approaching the room's dresser, she eased open the lowest drawer and searched under a stack of bed sheets. Out came a fat book, the size my mom sometimes put on our coffee table. When I saw the title, my eyes expanded.

The Nature of Sexuality.

On the cover, a black and white photo showed a man and a woman hugging. I could tell they had no clothes on, although their private parts weren't showing.

"Oh my gosh!" I whispered.

Caroline giggled. She glossed over the text at the beginning and opened to a full-page photo. A man and a woman lay naked on a bed.

In this picture, their privates *were* showing.

I felt my cheeks flush with warmth. "What is this doing here?" I asked.

"My mom bought it to teach me about sex," she said. "She showed it to me once, then stored it in here."

My eyes opened wide enough to twitch. "Are you serious?"

"Yeah, my parents believe that kids should learn stuff like this at home. And the right name for things. Like a penis," she said, pointing at the next page.

I stared at the nude photos. My own body stirred below the belt in a way that I'd only recently become familiar with. For the last few months, my mornings had included a strange and pleasant swelling *down there*. Sometimes, if it happened during the night, I'd wake and stand at the toilet for drowsy, torturous minutes, waiting for the hardness to recede so I could pee.

I hadn't talked about this with anyone. I definitely didn't want it to happen around Caroline – a *girl* – but I didn't know how to stop it.

My discomfort grew.

As a diversion, I flipped the page. A close-up displayed the woman's face, lips pursed, near the man's crotch. I had no doubt what part of him she meant to kiss.

"Oh – my – gosh."

Her mom had shown this book to her? Mounting tension above my belt stifled the excitement below. Caroline was only eight. That seemed too young to be learning this stuff. I was eleven. I could handle it better.

We paged through the rest of the book, showing the woman's pregnant belly, then a child, and finally a whole family – mom, dad, boy, girl – all in black-and-white nakedness. My body relaxed as the pictures became less sexual. The people still paraded across the pages without clothes but, by the end, all four of them stood in the living room hugging as a family.

Caroline closed the book and nestled it back among the spare sheets. We returned to our search for secret passageways but, in the pit of my stomach, I struggled to shake the feeling that we'd done something wrong.

Maybe Adam, my best friend at my new Catholic school, would have some words of wisdom about *The Nature of Sexuality*.

???

After the boards-in-the-bed incident, Mom had talked to Dad about switching me from public school to Saint Michael's, a Catholic grammar school in Arcadia, two towns away. Over a glass of scotch whiskey, he'd pronounced that *it seemed like a proper decision considering my scholastic aptitude and propensity toward religion*. Drinking Dar talk.

Preparations began in earnest. At Saint Michael's, boys were required to wear blue or brown slacks and white, gold, or blue golf-knit shirts – all the approved colors.

Mom took me to Country Clothiers, a clothing store in town where she knew the clerk. He was a short guy with closely cropped brown hair. I didn't like the way his hair and side burns hugged his head like a helmet or the fact that he talked only to my mom.

"Saint Michael's, huh?" he said with a crooked smile. His inflection on *huh* sounded conspiratorial. "C'mon back here and we'll find something for you, Mrs. Gerard." I trailed behind and endured the next twenty minutes as they selected various clothing combinations, which I dutifully modeled. We left with two corduroy pants and five long-sleeve shirts, enough to rotate through a week's worth of learning.

That night, Mike and I lay in our shared bedroom. After we turned out the lights, he spoke into the darkness. "You know, some of the teachers at Saint Michael's are *nuns*," he said, his tone seeking a reaction.

I turned toward the sound of his voice. "You mean like in *The Sound of Music*?" Ever since I'd seen the film at the Macedon theater, I'd played the album on our living room turntable, singing all the songs at the top of my lungs. *Climb Every Mountain. Sixteen Going on Seventeen. How Do You Solve a Problem Like Maria. The Sound of Music* was my favorite movie.

My brother laughed. "Yeah, like *The Sound of Music*. So you better behave or maybe they'll make you sing in front of the whole class or something." He paused for emphasis. "They might even be able to send you to confession if you do something bad. I bet Father McFarland even gets a report on what happens there. G'night," he finished quickly. I heard him turn over and pull the covers taut.

I tried to fall asleep, but my mind worked. *Would the nuns have rulers to whack kids' knuckles, like everybody always joked about? When I entered the confessional at Saint Patrick's, would Father McFarland know my sins before the wooden door slid open?* Underneath my pajamas, my stomach clenched.

I finally drifted off, praying that, if the nuns *were* like the movie, they'd be more like the fun young ones who stuck up for Maria, not the crusty older nuns who sang about what a pest she was and how she was late for everything.

The night before school began, I knelt at my bedside. "God, please be with me tomorrow at my new school." I added my regular signoff, inspired by my oldest brother's troubles. "And please cure all the sick people around the whole world."

The next morning, instead of leaving me to ride the bus I'd normally take, Dad drove me to Saint Michael's in our brown-paneled station wagon. He said he wanted to meet the principal.

Like the nuns at my new school, my father also had a *Sound of Music* counterpart. The first time I'd seen the movie, I noticed his resemblance to Herr Zeller, the cranky Nazi who chased the von Trapps from their home. It wasn't a perfect match. Herr Zeller was angry all the time; Dad only ranted, cursed, or threw things sometimes. Today, he seemed in a good mood.

I looked across the bench seat at my father. Six feet tall, his bald head nearly scraped the ceiling of our station wagon. Normally he wore tan work pants from Country Clothiers, but today he had his church slacks on. *Because we're meeting nuns*, I guessed.

After a thirty-minute drive, we pulled into a parking lot attached to a two-story brick building. The school was the same red color as Big Brick, but shorter and fatter. Two rows of metal-framed windows covered the front. Slightly off center, double doors under a short awning invited us with a sign: WELCOME – ALL VISITORS REPORT TO SCHOOL OFFICE. We entered and followed more signs. It was early, so there weren't many people around.

A woman with graying hair sat in the school's office behind a modest wooden desk. A plaque identified her as "Sr. Joyce McGinn, Principal." She stood and extended her right hand to my dad.

"I'm Sister Joyce," she said. "Welcome to Saint Michael's." She wore a knitted sweater and navy skirt. I was surprised, having expected the black-and-white outfits from the movie. The gray sweater was *not* an approved color, I noted.

She and Dad hit it off right away. She explained what a fine Catholic institution Saint Michael's was and how she believed in character building combined with religious education. "Some of our instructors belong to the Sisters of Saint Joseph," she said. "The rest are lay teachers."

Sister Joyce led us across the hall. "Sister Helen," she called into an open classroom, where strains of guitar music filtered out.

"Hello, Joyce!" A younger version of the principal appeared, also in regular lady-wear. Sister Helen had short brown hair and matching brown clogs. She removed a guitar strap from over her shoulder. Now we were closer to *Sound of Music* territory.

"Welcome!" she shook my father's hand enthusiastically, her eyes showing excitement. "It's a pleasure, Mr. Gerard."

"We've heard lots of good things about Saint Mike's," Dad started. "This is *The Caboose*," he continued, nudging me forward with his left hand. I felt warmth rise in my cheeks as I shook Sister Helen's hand. My father winked at the nun. "If he doesn't stay in line, you give me a call."

"We've got a special hotline just for that purpose," she replied with mock intensity.

I stood in embarrassed silence.

"Greg, the other kids will gather on the playground in a little bit, but you can wait in the classroom if you like. When they come in, I'll introduce you," she said, smiling at me.

"Okay, Sister."

She shook my dad's hand a final time. "Take care, Caboose," he said and left. I followed Sister Helen across the hall. She rested her guitar against the nearby wall and sat at a desk where small piles of paper flanked her on either side. Her brown clogs poked out at me from beneath a forest-green skirt.

"Greg, why don't you take some time to pick out a seat," my new teacher said.

While she worked her papers, I walked the rows, finally selecting a desk on the window side of the room. Lifting the desk lid, I unpacked school supplies I'd purchased the previous week: a notebook; some Super Friends pencils.

I looked out the window and saw that kids had begun to gather in the parking lot. They were running in a spiral, playing a game I didn't recognize.

My stomach knotted. As a distraction, I pulled out my notebook and supplies. I decided to make up a story, something mysterious that a Catholic schoolboy in Arcadia might encounter. Selecting a Superman pencil, I toyed with different titles. *The Murdered Maid. Father McFarland's Fatal Mistake. The Clue in the Nun's Habit.*

Before I'd settled on any one, a bell in the hall jangled furiously, making my stomach flip again. The children outside the window disappeared around the corner of the school. Sister Helen stood. "Well, Greg, are you ready?"

"Yeah," I said, my voice dropping off too soon.

The teacher smiled. "It won't be so bad. They're good kids."

A couple of minutes later, children began filing into the classroom. They rushed to claim seats as though they knew exactly where they wanted to sit. Several of them glanced over at me, then continued to talk to each other.

A thin, brown-eyed boy sat at the desk immediately behind me. Taking a deep breath, I turned around and smiled. "I'm Greg."

He returned the smile. "I'm Adam."

"I live in Macedon," I offered.

Adam's eyes lit up. "We drive through there sometimes on our way to the city!"

"That's neat," I said, not sure where to go next.

Adam took the lead. "So whattya think of Saint Mike's?"

I shrugged my shoulders and leaned closer, lowering my voice. "I thought the nuns would wear those black and white robes like in *The Sound of Music.*"

Adam chuckled and nodded. "That was a good movie!"

Sister Helen interrupted our conversation. "Welcome, Children. Let's start with the roll."

I turned back to the front of the class, now more excited than anxious. *I made my first Catholic school friend!* As our teacher read names, I worked on my detective skills, using my Superman pencil to scratch each kid's first name in my notebook. The top of my list read *Adam*.

???

"Honey, run back to the laundry room and grab me a bag of sugar off the storage shelves," Mom said, winking at me. "I think we might be needing a batch of fudge this afternoon."

Whistling, I wove my way through Big Brick's back hallway. I reached the laundry room and looked through the open doorway at the construction equipment inside Gram's apartment. My whistling stopped.

My grandmother had passed away at eighty four, a year earlier. During the night, an artery in her chest had ruptured. She'd tried to come get us, but only made it to the double doors between her garage apartment and Big Brick's laundry room.

My brother, Paul, had been the one to discover her. He'd gotten up to go to the bathroom in the night and somehow heard her moaning from all the way upstairs. Another miracle for our family stories.

Dad rode in the ambulance with Gram in a pre-dawn race toward Strong Hospital, the same place where Paul had all his brain surgeries. But she'd suffered too much internal damage; she died on the way.

Now, a year after Gram's death, my parents were overloaded with debt and my dad was out of work. The swimming pool, Gram's apartment, and even Catholic school I supposed, had cost a lot of money.

To support the family, Dad engineered a two-part strategy. He would open a mini grocery store, like he'd run years before. And Mom would open a family-style adult care home right inside our house. We kids would help with both businesses.

The same guys who converted the garage the first time around had returned two days ago, tearing apart Gram's quarters at a furious pace.

Stepping over drop cloths and nail cans, my eyes avoided the spot where Gram had fallen. It had been more than a year, but I still felt an elusive emptiness, like I'd buried a treasure and lost the map to find it. I grabbed the sugar from the laundry shelves and rushed back to our kitchen to make fudge. Very soon, I felt the soothing chocolate fill me.

???

Saint Michael's School had a church-like regularity that appealed to me. Above the blackboard at the front of each classroom, a speaker and crucifix hung side-by-side. Every morning in homeroom, the speaker popped to life with the ringing of a hand bell. We all knew it was Sister Joyce next to a microphone in her office. Adam and I stood from our chairs with the rest of the students and began morning prayers. The Our Father, the Hail Mary, the Glory Be, the Apostle's Creed, the Pledge of Allegiance. Our daily litany.

Two priests, Father Fredricks and Father Deckman, managed Saint Michael's Church right across the street from our school. The older, Father Fredricks, reminded me of a tired, elderly wizard, his expression appearing slightly sour at the altar. His off-white robe hung languid at his sides. *He looks like he'd rather be taking a nap,* I thought, whenever he presided over our school-day functions. His eyes sometimes closed as we performed the motions of Mass: *Stand* during the gospel reading. *Sit* during the homily. *Kneel* during the consecration.

The younger priest, Father Deckman, was more like Father McFarland. He joked with our teachers. I liked it whenever he visited our classroom. We were taught to stand when he, or any adult, entered the room.

"Good afternoon, Father Deckman," we'd chorus, jumping up from our seats when the priest dropped by for an unscheduled visit.

A trimmed brown mustache added warmth to his face. Thick glasses in black frames perched on his nose, but they didn't hide the squinty twinkle at the corner of his eyes. Like my mom, Father Deckman often laughed.

"Good afternoon, boys and girls," he'd motion for us to sit. He'd talk with Sister Helen, then stop to chat with us for a bit.

Adam and I stood outside Saint Michael's during recess, playing our favorite game, Truth or Dare. We students had a twenty-minute midday break each day. During bad weather, Sister Helen would keep us inside and play the guitar for us, songs like *This Land is Your Land* or *Turkey in the Straw*. Today, it was sunny. After lunch, we all marched outside.

It was chilly enough that I'd worn my winter coat, a brown corduroy that zipped all the way to my chin. Adam wore a flat gray jacket that reached nearly to his knees. We wandered the parking lot, engrossed in conversation.

Even though I'd only known him a few months, I already considered him my best friend. He liked all the things I liked: *The Hardy Boys*, *The Bionic Woman*, even searching for secret passageways with me and Caroline. As we walked side by side, without thinking, I stuck out my arm and linked it through his. He offered no objection.

"Truth or dare," I challenged him.

The object of the game was simple but perilous: choose *truth* and have to answer *any* question; choose *dare* and have to perform *any* feat. When we played at his house, the kids in his neighborhood sometimes asked for tough things, like showing your underwear or licking the sidewalk. Here, in the shadow of Saint Michael's tall steeple, dares were somewhat restrained.

"Truth," he answered.

I thought for a minute. "Of all the people in the whole world, who's your best friend?"

"Well..." he stalled. "Can I count people who are bionic?" We laughed. "You know it's you, Greg. That was a dumb question. I should have picked da—"

"What are you two girls talkin' about?" Brent, a pudgy blond kid, interrupted. He wore a light windbreaker – even though the air was crisp enough to snow. A football remained cocked in his right hand, paused for a forward pass. Adam and I stopped our conversation abruptly.

"None of your beeswax," I offered, my mind scrambling for an appropriate response.

Adam was sharper. "We'd explain it to you, but we don't have all afternoon."

Brent sneered and turned back to his game, offering one final dig. "Have a nice *stroll*."

We moved away, but I was now acutely aware of my left arm linked through Adam's. I didn't want to pull it away, granting Brent some victory, but I was relieved when the bell rang.

"What a jerk he is," I complained, as we unlatched our arms and lined up at the doors for Sister Helen to retrieve us.

"Just ignore him, Greg. Hurry, ask me truth or dare again, before Sister gets here."

"Truth or dare," I said quickly.

"Truth," he said. "Now ask me what Brent is."

"Okay, what is Brent?"

Adam face turned mock-stony. "I am compelled to tell the truth. Brent is a big fat goober!" He burst into giggles.

I joined my friend's laughter.

???

Adam often stayed overnight at Big Brick, most recently joining me to watch the workmen install carpets and paint walls. In less than a month's time, Big Brick's living room and Gram's apartment were carved up to accommodate four private rooms for elderly adults.

My father prepared a brochure to attract customers. *Independent living in a family atmosphere* was printed on the cover, along with a black and white picture of Big Brick from the end of the winding drive. In the photo, it looked like a mansion from *Gone With The Wind*.

People began to show up to view Big Brick's adult care home. Grown-ups with their elderly parents made appointments to tour the freshly painted rooms. One by one they signed papers and checked their relatives in. Soon all four rooms were occupied.

A retired farmer from Palmyra now lived in my grandmother's bedroom. In my mind, I heard her yell *Good night shirt!* in response. His presence might have even earned a balled fist and a "*Smella that, Brother!*"

I quickly learned our borders' routine: three meals a day, a weekly bath, a person on hand to help in a crisis. "How much money are we making for all this work?" I asked Mom while she cleaned a pile of dishes.

She continued to face the sink, her familiar spot. "It costs them fifteen dollars a day. Your dad was right. It's the best way to make this place pay for itself." I couldn't see her expression, but my detective skills sensed a secret lurking in her tone. *She doesn't agree.*

It felt strange, having these interlopers in our home. I missed Gram. I missed our huge living room, where I'd danced to *The Sound of Music* soundtrack. Back when Big Brick housed only family.

My only comfort lay in the hope that one of these *Old People*, as we'd begun to call them, might be keeping a secret: a hidden will, a murderous nephew. I stayed vigilant as we served meals, delivered mail, and did laundry for the four boarders. Nothing out of the ordinary surfaced.

Instead of promoting adventure or intrigue, most of them sat quietly in their bedrooms watching TV. Occasionally, one would make the trek out to our kitchen, asking when dinner would be ready.

Meals were a big focus for the Old People. Mom made the food warm and appealing. "It's all they've got to look forward to," she said one night, doling out huge piles of mashed potatoes and gravy onto four plates.

I helped her carry the tray, calling the adults to my Gram's kitchen table. The same place I'd sat and eaten maple walnut ice cream while my grandmother told her tragic stories.

The trade-off – my grandmother for these elderly strangers – felt like rocks in the pit of my stomach.

Mom and I walked back to our end of Big Brick, taking the route through the revised living room. "We went from having the biggest living room I ever saw to having the smallest," I said out loud. The disdain in my voice was palpable.

Mom let out a long breath, then looked at me. "It's not so bad, Greg," she said finally. "Offer it up."

???

Our new grocery store, just a ten-minute drive from our house, opened shortly after the adult care home. Dad had owned and operated a mom-and-pop store very successfully back in the Fifties. After a run in local politics in the Sixties, he was ready to return to what he knew.

The first candy delivery for *Gerard's Grocery* – the name Dad selected for the store – arrived a week before we opened for business. Cases of my favorite candy bars lined the wall just inside the front door.

"Go ahead," Dad invited us on our first visit. "Take what you'd like." When he was in a good mood, like today, my dad could be an okay guy. What bothered my stomach most days was the uncertainty of when fun would turn to fury. I worked to learn the shifting signals, watching his facial expressions and monitoring his tone. As an aspiring detective, it seemed like an important skill to master.

Mike, Anne, and I dug into the candy boxes like we'd been set loose at the Wonka factory. I loaded my pockets with packets of M&Ms. The enormity of owning a store – to have this much access to sweets, to maybe catch shoplifters in the act – was a welcome distraction after the arrival of the Old People.

???

In addition to looking after our elderly boarders, Mom helped with Dad's store. Dad nicknamed her *The Booker* because she managed everything in our lives: Old People meals, the Gerard's Grocery work schedule, family vacations – and all the money from both my parents' businesses.

The Booker waited up for Dad to arrive each night so she could tally Gerard's Grocery's cash. My father carried it home from the store in a small brown sandwich bag. She'd count the money on her bed at night, then stow it the next morning in the second drawer of her desk, adding it to the checks she received for the Old People's room and board. Whenever we needed money for groceries, movies, or any other expense, Mom sent us into her office to raid the second-drawer down.

As a general rule, we kept this a secret from our dad. He often complained that our family spent too much money.

"Were you busy today, Darwin?" she asked as he handed her the bag at night. I sensed from my Dad's recent downturn in mood and more frequent visits to the liquor cabinet that this store's launch was less successful than the previous one.

"Not awfully," he replied, heading into the kitchen table for a late-night snack or a glass of scotch – or both.

The system worked well when Dad arrived before Mom went to bed. If she was already upstairs, she worried about yelling down from the second floor asking him to toss the bag of money up to her. She thought someone might overhear, even though Big Brick's closest neighbor was a quarter of a mile away.

One night he didn't get home until eleven. Mom stood at the top of the stairs, Dad at the bottom. "*Darwin, toss up the money,*" she used her best stage whisper. I could hear her clearly from my bedroom.

"For God's sakes, Mom, I can't hear you!" he yelled.

My stomach tightened like it always did when he raised his voice.

"Someone might be listening at the window!" she spoke a tiny bit louder. "Toss up the *YOU KNOW WHAT!*"

"Awww, bunk," he growled. I heard the small bag hit the landing at the top of the stairs. The ritual was complete. I turned over in my bed as I heard my mother's steps back to her bedroom, mingled with the clink of bottles from the kitchen below.

The next morning, I joined my parents at the breakfast table. "We'll use code, Darwin," Mom said as I sat down.

My head snapped around. *Code was something the Hardys would use.* "For what?" I asked her.

"So your dad and I can talk about the bag of money at night without crooks understanding."

I glanced at my father. He stirred sweetener into his coffee, his face portraying annoyed skepticism. I shifted in my chair. Annoyance sometimes became anger.

"So what's it gonna be, Booker?" he said.

Mom continued. "I'll ask you if you have the two fried eggs and that will mean the money."

"*Two fried eggs?*" Dad looked at me and smirked. I giggled as the tension that had threatened my stomach dissipated. "You couldn't come up with something better than that? Why don't you just ask me if I brought the Pal-Mac marching band home with me?"

She laughed. "Two fried eggs will be just fine. We'll have our own little family secret."

???

I loved it when my school friends slept over, but since Saint Mike's was over thirty minutes away, it was tough to get some parents to agree to the round trip. During the school year, my bus driver allowed Saint Michael's friends to ride home with me on the

51

bus. In the summertime, I had to negotiate trips for Adam. I relied on Paul for transportation.

Adam visited on a scorching summer day. Humidity hung in the air like a fog, so we headed for the swimming pool behind the garage. Despite the heat, the first leap into the water was a frigid shock.

"Ahhhh!" I surfaced, screaming melodramatically. Adam laughed.

We practiced different running dives, tearing across the lawn and flipping over the edge. "Let's make a whirlpool," I suggested.

"Okay."

We circled the perimeter, pushing against the water. The whirlpool picked up speed, so we relaxed and floated. Adam hung close, his bare body and goose flesh bumping into my thigh. I shoved him away.

"Whattya wanna do now?" I asked as we drifted, our faces just above the water's surface. I could see his teeth beginning to chatter from the cold.

"I dunno," he said, curling his blue lips and spitting water directly into my face. I laughed and began to wrestle with him.

When the pool-water's chill had settled into my own body, I crawled onto the deck and lay in the warm sun. Adam joined me. I could hear his steady breathing as his bare chest rose and fell.

"Truth or dare?" I asked suddenly.

"Truth," he said.

"What's your middle name?" I asked, knowing he didn't want to share it. He tilted his head toward me, squinting through one eye in the bright sun. "You *have* to answer, those are the rules," I said.

"Leonard," he said, staring at me, as if gauging my reaction. "It was my grandfather's name."

"That's not so bad." I smiled. "Your turn."

"Truth or dare?" he asked. I drank the sun's heat into my cool skin.

"Truth."

Adam thought for a long time, then spoke. "Do you ever get a boner?"

"What?"

"You heard me."

I lay there considering the unexpected question.

"Yeah," I finally answered.

Neither of us spoke. We hadn't uncovered anything like this while exploring the house, or the barn, or any of the two hundred acres around Big Brick. My mind started to wash with possibilities, questions I could ask, things I might dare him to do. It felt naughty.

And private.

And good.

"Truth or dare," I said finally.

"Truth."

"Do *you* ever get a boner?"

"Yeah, almost every morning."

The air seemed electric, as though the humidity of the day had somehow produced an arc between our bodies. He continued.

"Truth or dare?"

I lay quiet, trying to control my excitement. "Dare."

Adam didn't hesitate. "Jump into the pool naked."

I sat up and looked at him. He continued to squint through one eye. By now, the droplets of pool water had evaporated from our skin, replaced with sweaty beads.

"Okay."

I stood and hitched my thumbs into the top edge of my suit.

"Wait a minute." Adam got up and walked around the pool to the opposite side. He sat on the metal rim, looking at me. "Okay, now."

I walked to the corner of the garage and peered around. Nobody – my family, the Old People, or one of their visitors – was in sight. Back on the deck, I peeled off my bathing trunks. My excitement exposed, I ran forward and leapt into the cool water.

Adam didn't move as I surfaced and swam back to the deck, grabbing my suit and putting it on underwater.

"Truth or dare," I said.

He looked straight at me. "Dare."

"*You* jump into the pool naked, just like I did," I repeated, making sure not to misspeak, to give him some way to wiggle out of it. He stood on the metal rim and took off his trunks. He was as excited as I was.

Tossing his suit into the pool, he jumped, creating a huge splash as his body hit the surface. I watched as he retrieved his suit and put it on.

We continued daring each other for a long while, inventing different ways to jump into the pool naked: flipping, leapfrogging, finally toppling in like a felled tree.

Afterwards, back in the house and fully clothed, neither of us mentioned the new twist in our game.

RUNAWAY PLAN: Cincinnati/Days Three—Twelve (1984)

The Cincinnati rooftop became my daily retreat. Each morning, I climbed the staircase, my book bag stuffed with a beach towel and my Sheena tapes. The big-city pigeons didn't seem intimidated by my presence; they simply moved aside as I spread my towel.

I brought the mail up as well. Letters had begun to flow between Rochester and Cincinnati. My high school friends. My siblings. Everybody was keeping in touch. Even my brother, Mike, wrote me again. Drinking Dar penned yellow legal pages filled with flowing phrases like 'Your mother and I commend your decision to attend a Jesuit institution.'

I carried pen and pad to the roof, eagerly writing to them from my sunny perch, sharing all sorts of thoughts that rambled through my brain – with the exception of the one subject not even crooks could beat out of me.

Chapter Five: Gregory Gerard, First Investigator (1978)

"GO ON IN," the guy at the counter grabbed our money and waved us by. I held the brown paper sack low at my side. To the casual observer, the bag contained popcorn I'd brought for Adam's and my third theater viewing of *Star Wars*. People didn't know that underneath the popcorn lay my battery-powered tape recorder. That I was executing a clandestine plan.

I'd decided to record *Star Wars* earlier that day. Adam and I both loved the movie; I looked forward to playing back the tape and enjoying the story again and again. Like an old-fashioned radio play.

I knew it was illegal to record movies in general, but my great love for *Star Wars* helped me rationalize that I wouldn't be committing a sin. Pushing thoughts of Father McFarland and the confessional aside, I focused on the technical setup.

Like a detective on a case, I laid the recorder across the bottom of the paper sack and threaded the external mike down my sleeve. *It would work, but how would I get the bag into the theater without attracting attention?* Heading to the kitchen, I pulled out the huge pot Dad used to make sauce, filled the bottom with butter, and poured a whole bag of popcorn kernels in. In a few minutes, enough corn had popped to cover the recorder and provide a snack before the show.

My brother, Paul, dropped us off at a movie house in Rochester where *Star Wars* had played for the last six months. I had the bag of popcorn clutched inconspicuously at my hip, but I needn't have worried. Nobody questioned me.

The theater was already crowded. We found seats near the back, right in the middle. I surreptitiously placed the popcorn bag on the floor at my feet, clutching the mike in my left hand.

I was ready – but we were early.

My arm itched. I stuck my finger carefully up the sleeve and tried to scratch without disrupting the setup. Adam chatted amiably as I tried to focus on his words. "So if it says 'a long time ago in a galaxy far, far away', do you think some people believe this actually happened?"

My eyes surveilled every entrance. "I dunno," I said. *What if security hauled me in?* "I think it's just supposed to be like *Star Trek*." I paused and readjusted the popcorn bag between my legs. "You know, that it *could* happen."

Adam punched my arm. "Just act *normal*, for cripes sake, and nobody's gonna know about the tape recorder."

"Shhhhhh!" I cautioned him. "I don't want anyone to catch on!" Thankfully, the lights dimmed, plunging the seats and my popcorn bag into darkness. I switched on the recorder. The opening script scrolled across the screen. I whispered it word-for-word into my sleeve.

The sound of laser blasters shook the theater. Holding my left arm near my head to give the microphone the best sound, I tried to appear casual. C3PO and R2D2 came onto the screen and the dialogue began.

I shifted uncomfortably, looking toward the aisles. *If they come for me, will I have time to get away?* I glanced at the girl next to me. *Would she suspect something and turn me in before the movie ended?*

It was useless. I didn't have the nerve to pull it off. I shut off the recorder and consoled myself with popcorn.

Twenty minutes later, Obi wan Kenobi had just introduced himself to Luke Skywalker when the guy in front of Adam reached over the back of his seat and grabbed my shirt collar. He yanked, pulling my face within an inch of his.

I'm not taping anymore! flashed through my mind as my heart triphammered inside my chest.

He stared at me in the dark. His voice was low, gravelly, and thoroughly serious. "Are you kicking my daughter's seat on purpose?" he growled.

"No," I squeaked out.

"Well make sure you aren't," he said and released his grip.

I fell back into my chair. I pulled my legs as far away from the seat in front of me as I could manage. My hand groped for popcorn to squelch the panic in my stomach.

"What was that all about?" Adam said quietly.

I pressed my mouth directly against his ear. "He thought I was kickin' his daughter's seat," I whispered as my pulse slowed.

"What a jerk," my friend muttered in my defense.

We watched the rest of the movie without interruption. I felt ravenously hungry, but I left enough popcorn in the bag to cover the recorder, in case I was searched as we left the theater.

???

"He has vat I callt a nervus stumak," our town's German doctor explained to my mom with his thick Albert Einstein accent. He poked at my abdomen some more. "Give him von half of dese pills vhenever his stumak hurts." He scribbled on a white square of paper and handed it to my mother.

My stomach troubles had snuck up on me. Without warning, an anxious pain would begin low in my gut, then work its way up to grip the whole area above my belt. At first Mom fed me Milk of Magnesia.

"To sweeten your stomach," she said, pulling out the familiar blue bottle with a dollop of dried paste leaking from the cap. Next to me she set the *spitty basin*, a beige plastic tub Paul used for quick vomiting when he had pressure headaches. I stared at it, willing myself to recover.

After the doctor's diagnosis, we filled the prescription and went home. The nervous stomach pills took up residence on the kitchen windowsill. Every time I washed my hands, I looked at the small cardboard box and wondered why nobody else in my family had to take them. *What was wrong with me?*

I didn't know the answer but on days when my insides felt achy and anxious, I took out a knife and split one of the tiny pucks in half. Despite their bitter taste going down, within a half hour, I always felt better.

???

On a Friday afternoon, while a late-winter storm raged against the metal-framed windows of our classroom, Mrs. Stirpe, our sixth-grade teacher for Reading and Health, handed out an assignment on public speaking. She was one of the lay teachers, younger than Sister Helen and, in contrast to the nuns at Saint Michael's, Mrs. Stirpe often wore pants and told us funny stories about her kids.

For homework, we were supposed to search through newspapers and bring in an article to read aloud. Due the following Monday.

I was excited at the thought of standing in front of my classmates reading a gut-wrenching story. Maybe about a detective who located somebody's long-lost relative. Or maybe a priest who saved a maid from a three-alarm rectory fire. It could happen.

The next day, I scanned the stack of newspapers Dad kept on the floor by his kitchen chair. No missing relative. No cooked maid. I settled for an article about the resurgence in popularity of *The Lord of the Rings*; we'd just read a chapter from *The Hobbit* in our reader.

I rushed to Reading class Monday morning, article in hand. It wasn't the drama I'd imagined, but nonetheless, I was ready to impress. In the classroom, most of the kids were gathered around Adam's desk, sniggering. "What's up?" I tried to break in. Mrs. Stirpe called us to order before he had a chance to reply. The lesson began.

"Who will go first?" she asked. I raised my hand, but several of the boys in the first row shouted "Adam!"

She made her decision. "Okay, Adam, go ahead."

He strode to the front of the class and stood behind the wooden podium, his shoulders barely visible over its Catholic-school bulk.

"*Church Says NO To Gays*," he read the title.

Laughter erupted in the classroom.

My stomach flip-flopped. *How could he have picked something so naughty to read?* I looked to our teacher for direction.

"Alright, that's enough," Mrs. Stirpe commanded the class. "Adam, continue."

"*Despite the reforms of Vatican II, the Roman Catholic Church holds firm on its condemnation of sexual activity outside of marriage. The Church posits that homosexuals who are incurable should be treated with understanding and judged with prudence. Additional church guidelines described masturbation as a seriously disordered act.*" My best friend burst into giggles, unable to continue.

"Adam, sit down," Mrs. Stirpe instructed, bringing his assignment to a close. Snorts continued from several corners of the room.

I whispered to Adam when he sat back at his desk. "Why did you read that?"

He shrugged his shoulders. "Because it was funny, man!"

???

It was Sunday and a spring rain beat down on Big Brick. I stayed in my bedroom after Mass reading *The Clue in the Diary*, a Nancy Drew novel. In the story, Nancy found a mysterious diary that helped her solve the case. I read all afternoon.

Closing the book, I leaned back on the pillow and thought about Nancy, the titan-haired detective, and her diary habits. *What was it like to have a chronicle of daily events?* A journal was something a real detective could use to record the clues he encountered. Besides, I had a new secret I wanted to share with somebody.

61

Hanging over the edge of the mattress, I pawed through the mess under my bed – candy wrappers, Superman comic books, a piece of dried orange peel – finally locating the small spiral notebook I knew was there. I grabbed a pencil out of my nightstand drawer and opened to the first page. I scribbled *5/7/78* across the top of the page, then looked at it.

That wasn't a good start. If people discovered my diary a hundred years in the future, they wouldn't know whether it meant May of *1978* or *2078*. This was for posterity. Besides, detectives were expected to keep exact notes.

Erasing, I started again.

Sunday, May 7, 1978
Dear Diary,
Father Deckman took some of us Saint Mike's students to Sacred Heart Cathedral in Rochester today. The Bishop said Mass! When I saw him standing up there, a thrill went through me.

I haven't told anybody this, but I think God wants me to be a priest.

Sometime in the past couple of months the idea had sprouted inside my head. Now, here was my secret on paper for the first time. I read it again.

I knew that my mom, Sister Helen, and certainly God would be happy with my decision. To be a priest like Father Deckman – not Father Fredricks. To wear the sacred robes and offer Mass for the sins of the world. To be God's representative on this Earth. I knew Jesus would be pleased when I announced my intention to follow in His footsteps.

For now, I kept the news a secret between me and my new detective's journal.

???

Mrs. Stirpe called us to attention in class on a Tuesday afternoon.

"Tomorrow during Health we're going to do something a little different," she said. "It's time for our sexual education studies." She looked across the students' attentive faces. "The girls will report to Sister Helen. The boys will stay here with me. We'll come back together at the end of the period."

"Wow," I whispered to Adam. "Sex ed!" I'd had the barn talk with my brother, Mike, four years earlier. Now, at twelve, I was ready to hear more details. To better understand his promises about girls and babies and desire.

Adam's face twisted. "Uh oh, I just thought of something," he whispered back. "We have Spanish tomorrow during Health!"

My thoughts raced as my gut constricted.

Two months earlier, Adam and I had signed up for Father Deckman's Spanish class. As a frequent missionary to Bolivia, he was fluent in the language and had arranged to teach willing students. The opportunity had appealed to me right away – I might be a missionary priest myself someday. Besides, speaking another language was like writing in code. A detective skill.

Now our decision worked against us. Not an official part of the curriculum, Spanish interrupted whatever course fell during that slot in our rotating Wednesday schedule. I liked spending time with my favorite Saint Mike's priest, but missing sex ed wasn't something I wanted to *offer up*.

"What are we gonna do?" Adam asked.

"We'll just come to Health. Maybe he won't notice that we're not in Spanish." My friend nodded in cautious agreement.

After school, I turned it over in my mind. *What if Father Deckman noticed our absence the next day? What if he kicked us out of Spanish class? What would he think of a kid who cared more about a sex class than spending time learning a missionary language? That was probably not the kind of kid God wanted for a priest.* My belly groaned. I headed to the kitchen for a nervous stomach pill before dinner.

The next day, Adam and I took our seats for Health with the rest of the boys. Mrs. Stirpe closed the classroom door and faced us. "Okay, guys, we're going to go through some important stuff but I want to lay down some ground rules. For starters, you don't need to giggle every time I hand out a diagram. Second, you don't need to discuss everything you hear today with the girls; this class is for you, they have their own class with Sister Helen. You'll all learn mostly the same things. Finally, I want you to feel free to ask any questions you need to. I'll answer anything that's appropriate."

Brent, the football player from the playground, raised his hand. "If they're learning the same thing, how come the girls aren't in here with us?"

Mrs. Stirpe shook her head and laughed. "Oh no, I'm not ready for that! We'll be fine with just the guys. Besides, boys usually have different questions than girls do, so I do it this way to make sure everybody's comfortable asking the questions they need to."

Our teacher began her talk while distributing mimeographed, hand-drawn diagrams of the male and female reproductive anatomy. I could tell she had created them herself; I recognized her handwriting on the various labels: the glans, the urethra. Clinical, but exciting.

She spoke at length about how the uterus and vagina were structured, then started into the male anatomy. A knock at the door interrupted her.

Father Deckman stepped through the doorway. "Hi Shirley!" he offered a cheerful greeting. "We have Spanish class right now. I think Adam and Greg have forgotten 'cause it rotates around a bit."

Mrs. Stirpe looked at Adam and me. I froze.

We'd hear no more about the penis today. Father Deckman's time was a commodity. He was a priest – not to mention a missionary – and he was doing us a favor by teaching us Spanish.

My face must have betrayed my inner turmoil. Mrs. Stirpe took Father's arm and led him into the hall. I heard her speak briefly, although her words were unintelligible from inside the classroom.

"Haw Haw Haw!" Father Deckman broke up loudly. He stuck his head back into the room. "Okay, boys, you can make it up next week."

My face prickled with embarrassment but I was too relieved to care. Mrs. Stirpe and Father Deckman had come through for us.

???

Summer arrived early. In response, my father expanded the hours Gerard's Grocery was open. My brother, Paul, worked there full time during the day. He'd had a successful run of health: no brain surgery for more than two years. My sisters, Kathy and Anne, and I helped out after school and on the weekends. I loved the easy access to all the food we stocked.

At work and at home, eating and reading became my regular pastimes – especially when my stomach felt jittery. The nervous stomach pills had finally run out; somehow, in the flurry of running our new family businesses, we'd never refilled the prescription. To quell my tensions, I ate whatever food I could find. My stomach never felt anxious when it was stuffed.

Along with platters of snacks, I consumed a cache of mystery books I found in Big Brick's attic: my mother's Agatha Christie paperbacks and a collection called *The Three Investigators*.

This new series captured my attention. Similar to the Hardy Boys or Nancy Drew, three boys worked at solving the mysteries they stumbled across. The First Investigator was Jupiter Jones, overweight and intellectual. I felt a quick kinship with him.

Second Investigator Pete did the leg work and Third Investigator Bob did the research. They were good sidekicks, but they weren't the brains of the trio. I wanted to be Jupiter, who pinched his lip to think and who stayed one step ahead of the crooks in *The Secret of Terror Castle*. Like me, he focused on food and clues with equal enthusiasm.

I loved the clever twists in *The Mystery of the Stuttering Parrot* and *The Secret of Skeleton Island.* When I'd read all of the Three Investigators books I found in our attic, I rode my bike to the Macedon library and checked out several more.

???

Saturday became my standard night at Gerard's Grocery. "It's The Caboose's shift," my dad said when I arrived. "Five to nine, rain or shine," he joked.

Our store carried all types of snack foods, which Dad allowed us to eat while we worked. Endless varieties of cookies, potato chips, ice cream, all free for the taking. After a few weeks of testing combinations, I settled on a regular Saturday night line-up: pretzel rods, plain M&Ms, and 7-UP. The perfect mix of salty and sweet with bubbly soda to wash it all down.

In addition to waiting on the counter or eating snacks, the job included stocking the shelves with products from the back storeroom. My favorite task quickly became filling the magazine rack. Each Saturday night, I spent time categorizing and arranging the books for maximum sales potential.

We stocked a wide selection: bestsellers like *TV Guide* and *People*, but also eclectic choices including *True Detective*, a periodical that told crime stories. I liked reading it; it reminded me of Gram's tales. Real life cases – with all the gritty details – and how detectives solved them.

We also sold comic books, which gave me easy access to *Superman*, *Wonder Woman*, and other favorites. On very slow nights, I brought a few behind the counter to read while I munched on my snacks.

Despite my efforts at convenient presentation, Dad groused that the magazines weren't earning their shelf space. I worried that he'd eliminate the rack altogether – but he chose a different approach. My father tacked an unexpected addition onto the magazine order, one with a higher profit margin.

Playboy.

When the first shipment arrived, I broke the plastic strap off the stack, feeling appropriate someday-to-be-a-priest disdain.

I didn't have a category on the shelves for *Playboy*. "Where do you want me to put this?" I yelled through the swinging door that led to the back room, holding up a copy.

Dad looked at me from his perch on the utility stool near the walk-in cooler. I liked it best when he headed right home after I arrived. More often, he hung around the storeroom, drinking cans of beer from the cooler as he sorted and priced groceries. He tried hard to provide a wide variety of products that people had enjoyed in his other, more successful store – but it was a lot of work.

My father regarded the *Playboy*. "We'd better keep them behind the counter," he decided, after a minute's pause. "We don't need those *honyocks* from the factory standing around reading that on their lunch hour." I recognized the word – one of Gram's strange terms for guys who hung out on street corners with nothing to do.

"Okay," I said, returning to the front. Clearing a section near the cigar rack, I displayed our store's newest magazine on the back counter. I stepped to the customer area and looked at it. From here, they could see the cover, but would have to ask to purchase a copy.

Perfect.

I maintained my detached disgust. If I'd been the least bit unsure about Caroline's *Nature of Sexuality* book, I was clear on *Playboy*. The *honyocks* desired it – and reading it was definitely a sin.

In a few weeks, the next shipment of *Playboy* arrived. I was alone at the store as I unpacked it; Dad had left for home right after I arrived. I broke through the binding strap and stared.

Pamela Sue Martin!

Adam and I loved TV's *Hardy Boys/Nancy Drew Mysteries*. The detectives we admired had come to life: Parker Stevenson with his intense sincerity and Sean Cassidy with his friendly smile.

Pamela Sue Martin played Nancy, my childhood detective heroine. The show was a regular part of my Sunday night lineup.

I couldn't believe it. Nancy Drew, who wore a lovely gown to the policeman's ball, who *always* helped people in trouble, stared back at me from the cover of *Playboy*. She wore nothing but a trench coat half-unbuttoned, a large Holmes-ian magnifying glass in her hands.

The M&M/pretzel/7-UP mixture gurgled in my belly. *What a crummy thing for her to do.* I wondered how much she revealed on the inside pages. Curiosity flushed over me.

What would Jesus think?

If I just looked at it clinically, trying to understand why she did this – if I didn't lust after her – would I have to report that to Father McFarland in confession? Jupiter Jones, my overweight detective hero, would investigate further.

A customer came in, interrupting my mental battle. I pushed the pile aside, covering it with a brown paper sack.

The rest of the evening, I worked it through in my mind. Boys were *supposed* to want to look at *Playboy*, everybody knew that. I thought about calling Adam, to talk it over. As I reached for the phone, I remembered the article he'd read in Mrs. Stirpe's class. *Church Says NO To Gays.* The memory of his nervous giggles made me place the receiver back in its cradle.

My mind wandered to the Saint Michael's playground. Brent, the football player who wore a spring jacket during winter's chill, would surely flip through the magazine without a second thought.

That did it. When nine o'clock approached, I sneaked *Playboy* into my backpack and waited for Paul to pick me up.

At home, I found a flashlight in the kitchen drawer and headed out to the barn. I hadn't been back to the secret room since the day Mike had shown it to me but, today, it seemed the perfect place to be alone with my *Playboy*.

Carefully negotiating the planks on the stage – more bravely than I had four years earlier – I climbed over the grain bin wall and made my way to the dirty floor below. The room was as Mike and I had left it: musty, pitch-black, and private.

Flashing the light around the space, I spied a flat wooden ledge near the back, large enough for me to sit. Scooping the dirt and pigeon droppings onto the floor, I coughed as dust rose about me. Holding the flashlight between my shoulder and left ear, I sat on the ledge and pulled *Playboy* from my backpack. I opened it on my lap. Circles of light danced across the shiny pictures.

I decided to turn through the magazine page by page – I knew I was *supposed* to be excited. Building some suspense before reaching Pamela Sue at the centerfold might help.

The article's title first caught my attention: *Nancy Drew Grows Up.* I stared at the pictures. In one, I could see her breasts under some silky see-through material. In another, my heroine sprawled naked across a chair, a velvet blanket barely covering her privates.

She *wasn't* Nancy. The Nancy Drew I knew would never do anything so sleazy. With a resigned disgust, I slammed the cover closed and stashed the magazine deep in my backpack.

As I made my way back across the stage, I heard the pigeons coo and murmur far above my head.

???

As mid-summer loomed, I got into the habit of wandering outside before bed, heading for the field behind the barn where my dog, Pete, and I had search for crooks when I was a kid. He still joined me for every excursion.

On a Friday in late July, I called Pete up from the cellar and began my nighttime trek. Just past the final crags of the farm roads, the corn stalks took on an edgy stillness in the dim moonlight.

I turned on the barn's silo light and pretended it was a beacon, maybe signaling an enemy's lair or a fellow detective's stronghold.

Hiking along a row of corn that brushed at my elbows, I passed the pond, its algae-thickened water barely visible. Crickets congregated there, performing a raucous concert. I kept going, using the tree line on my right as a guide.

My stomach, my limbs, my mind all relaxed, as though I'd eaten a Mexican sundae and settled back on my pillows with a new Three Investigators' book. The confused angst I felt about *Playboy*, about Adam's newspaper article, about my dad's unpredictable anger dissipated in the soft, summer breeze. I began to pray, thanking God for being alive.

After fifteen minutes of steady walking, I reached the base of the hill where Anne, Mike, and I had ridden the toboggan when we were younger. Where Caroline and I sometimes spread a blanket over the field grass and read mystery stories. Taking a deep breath, I jogged up. Pete leaped through the thick weeds behind me. Reaching the peak, I stopped and looked back.

Stars winked at me from every direction. In the distance, the barn's silo light beckoned me toward home.

Pete raced along the hill's slope chasing something unseen, then returned to my side. I sat down in the dewy vegetation to pet him. "Do you feel God out here?" I asked my dog. His tongue lapped at my face, acknowledging the question. I hugged him tightly to my body. "I sure do."

Jesus always surrounded me in the field at night, as palpable as the thin, crisp wafer that dissolved on my tongue each Sunday. I thought about how pleased He would be when I became a priest. Out loud, I began to sing. *Amazing grace, how sweet the sound, that saved a wretch like me.*

In the twinkling silence, without a physical touch, His warmth flooded me. My eyes filled with grateful tears.

I made the journey back to the barn slowly, savoring the stillness. I shut off the silo light and passed by the windows of the Old People – or *Opes*, as we now referred to them. Gram's bedroom, now the farmer's, was dark; he'd gone to bed. Mildred, our newest old lady who occupied Gram's former living room, was still awake.

Through the open curtains I saw her shut off the TV. Her pasty skin hung in rolls below the hem of her blouse. She stood, stretched, then began to undress, right in front of the window. I sensed she couldn't see me in the pitch-black night. Before I could decide whether it was wrong to peep, she undid her shirt and revealed two gangly breasts, stretched low, almost covering her swollen belly.

Nothing like Pamela Sue Martin.

As I watched, she grasped them and yanked upwards, as if to air out the area underneath. I turned away, my stomach lurching.

Back in my bedroom, I tried to recapture the feeling of priestly warmth I'd felt in the field, but the only image to fill my mind as I drifted off to sleep was Mildred tugging at her saggy bosom.

???

July brought Mormon season, the ten days when people from around the globe crowded our small towns. Followers of the Mormon faith came to see the Hill Cumorah Pageant, an outdoor play about the Palmyra roots of their religion.

Many historic sites were located within a mile of Gerard's Grocery. Joseph Smith's home – the childhood house of the religion's founder. The Sacred Grove – where he saw an angel. Hill Cumorah – where he discovered the Book of Mormon.

The event turned into a boom time for our new grocery store. For the duration of the pageant, we opened three counter slots to accommodate the traffic: Paul or Kathy using the cash register; me or Anne punching buttons on my Texas Instruments calculator; Dad adding figures on the back of a brown paper bag.

Mormon travelers seemed as hungry as I always was. The line of customers streamed out the door, all of them seeking caffeine-free snacks and alcohol-free drinks. They had more rules than Catholics did about what they could eat. I felt sorry for them; some of my favorite foods – like chocolate and cola – were on many of the tourists' blacklists.

The second-drawer down filled up as the two-fried-eggs sack came home each night packed with cash. My father's mood improved noticeably.

At Saint Pat's, Father McFarland gave his annual "I-never-met-people-I-admired-more-or-agreed-with-less" speech. I paid attention to this homily. With their stories of golden plates written in ancient code and a seer stone as a translation tool, the Mormon religion seemed more of a mystery than my own faith.

"Every Monday," Father intoned from the pulpit, "Mormon dads and moms and children gather together for Family Night. Wouldn't it be wonderful if we could adopt a practice like that in our own families? But the things they hold sacred—" He went on, emphasizing how Catholics could share some of the Mormon behaviors, but not their beliefs.

The throngs of tourists attracted all sorts of *hucksters*, as my dad called them. He rented booth space in Gerard's Grocery's parking lot to jewelry, tee-shirt, and Bible-on-tape vendors from Utah and other faraway places.

I kept my eyes peeled for mischief – maybe smuggled goods or a counterfeit ring – but during the ten-day event, nothing surfaced.

When the pageant came to a close, Paul offered to drive one of the Bible-on-tape guys to the airport. In addition to playing church organ, my brother had a passion for driving. When he wasn't busy at the store or church, his 1970 Oldsmobile was in constant motion. Our family, our friends – and sometimes even strangers – relied on my brother for a ride. The Bible-on-tape guy accepted Paul's offer.

I climbed into the backseat, hoping for an ice cream stop on the return trip. During the ride, after talking about the successful week in sales, the conversation somehow segued to the dire state of American culture.

"Yeah, it's a shame people today are just *shacking up* instead of getting married," my brother said, referring to some of our store's customers in the trailer park across the street. The disdain in his voice was palpable. "What happened to waiting until you got married?"

"It's the same in Texas, where ah'm from," the Bible-on-tape salesman agreed. "And on top a that, y'all have to read about *gays* in the newspaper, seems lahhk everyday."

"Now *there's* a perfectly good word that got ruined," Paul continued without losing his annoyed tone. "It used to be you could say something was gay and it meant something happy. Until they had to go and adopt it for the *gay movement*." He shook his head as his passenger nodded agreement.

Yeah, it's too bad America's headed downhill, I thought, wanting to share my big brother's conviction.

???

Between the store and the adult care home, our family's finances seemed to be improving. With the proceeds from the influx of Mormon tourists, Dad decided to take the family for a three-day vacation to Ocean City, Maryland. "Time to take the tribe to the ocean," he said to my mother over dinner.

The Booker arranged Gerard's Grocery and Old People coverage. The Thursday before we left, I pulled out my book bag and crammed my swimsuit, nose plugs, and beach towel into the largest section. Sorting through the selection of Three Investigators books on my bedroom windowsill, I saw a long white RV chug up the hill in front of our house. It pulled into our driveway.

Pete ran across the front lawn barking, chasing the huge vehicle around to the backyard. I raced down the stairs and followed.

My father emerged from the driver's seat. "Whattya think?" he smiled at me.

"Wow," I said. "Did you buy this?"

73

Dad laughed. "No, Greg, that'd cost more than what the Mormons brought in. I just rented it for the weekend. But I figured we ought to travel to the ocean in style."

Mom and Kathy came out of the back of the house. "Oh my God, Darwin!" my mother said.

He chuckled. "Start loadin' it up, Mom. It's the thirty-footer, so I figure we'll be able to fit the whole clan."

We pulled out the next morning at four thirty. Dad drove; my brothers, sisters, and Mom slept in the various beds throughout the camper. I rode beside my father in the passenger's seat, studying the Eastern States map in the glare of the small overhead light. My dad was more relaxed than I'd ever seen – he chattered happily about the store business, then talked with me for awhile about Saint Mike's. My stomach relaxed in kind.

Through the state of Pennsylvania, Mike spelled Dad in the driver's seat, then Dad took over again when we reached the Maryland border. I continued to study the map, looking for clues to our location.

After eight hours on the road, I detected a change in the sky to the east. It seemed deeper and richer – sunset rich – even though it was just past noon.

An unusual odor hit my nose. It smelled like the salmon loaf Mom baked for dinner on Fridays during Lent – mixed with the taste of salty pretzel rods, my Gerard's Grocery treat.

Between the raised beach houses, I caught a glimpse of pounding surf. "There's the ocean!" I yelled and pointed. We crowded the RV's left-hand windows. "Do you think there were ever any shipwrecks or buried treasure here?" I said to no one in particular.

My oldest sister, Molly, nodded and smiled. "Maybe, Greg. Maybe."

Mom had booked us three rooms at the Sheraton Fountainbleu, a fourteen-story hotel right on the beach. I dumped my book bag and suitcase into the boys' room and pulled on my bathing suit and nose plugs. Joining Mike, Anne, and Kathy at the elevator, we headed out for our first swim in the ocean.

The roar of the waves reminded me of Lake Ontario back home, where our family swam when I was little. Before we had the pool. Memories of Gram telling her stories over lakeside picnic lunches washed over me. I smiled at the recollection.

The wind kicked up on the open beach. Bits of sand pecked at my skin as we picked our way among the sun bathers to the water's edge. The air felt electric and soothing at the same time.

I stuck my foot into the foamy mix swirling near the shore, then yanked it back. "It's not as warm as it looks!" I yelled.

Mike stepped next to me. "It gets warmer the farther out you go," he said, giving me a shove.

I splashed forward into the deeper water as he laughed. I tried to be angry, but the warm sunshine and smell of coconut suntan lotion felt too good. Instead, I scooped cold water at him as he lunged past, diving directly into a wave. Anne and Kathy came in after us.

After a little while, Mom, Dad, Paul, and Molly joined us in the water. As a family, we stayed on the beach until dinnertime, alternating between riding the pounding waves and warming ourselves on the huge blankets we spread across the hot sand.

When we weren't on the beach, we spent most of the next two days exploring Ocean City's many restaurants and shopping centers. The first chance we got to break away from the rest of the family, Mike and I rode the bus to the boardwalk – block after block of shops that ended at an amusement park. Tourists jammed the wide walkway, more people than I'd ever seen back in Macedon and Palmyra, even during Mormon season. I kept my eyes low to concentrate on walking through the crowd without ramming into anyone.

Mike glanced at me and scrunched his brow. "Greg, *why* are you looking down when there's all these babes to check out?! And they're hardly wearing anything!"

Knives of fear stabbed at my insides. My anxiety, temporarily set aside for vacation, came rushing back over me like a wave. My gut sank with the crushing revelation that, even in this sunny, far-from-our-regular-experience atmosphere, my brother's admiration was still beyond my grasp.

For the duration of our ocean trip, I worked hard to stare at girls wearing bikinis, hoping he'd notice.

???

I continued to capture daily events in my journal. It seemed a great way to chronicle the details of my life.

Tuesday, August 8, 1978
We just got back from Ocean City, Maryland. I brought home sand and ocean water in two little bottles as a souvenir. I really, really want to go back sometime. Mike, Paul and I were trying to figure out how we could afford it. We might go next summer.

I've been really hungry lately. For fun, Molly, Mom and I added up all the calories we ate. I ate 6000 calories today!

Near the middle of August, when we picked out my school clothes at Country Clothiers, not only had I grown taller, my waist had expanded two sizes. The clerk with the helmet hair smirked as he rolled out the yellow measuring tape. "He's a growing boy, Mrs. Gerard, heh, heh," he said to my mom.

Hot shame poured into my cheeks. I knew what he meant. I was *fat.* I suddenly felt exposed, as if I were standing naked while he poked at my flabby gut and laughed. I couldn't wait to get out of the store.

When we got home, my stomach continued to jangle with nervous embarrassment. To silence the clamor, I piled a stack of pizza slices onto a plate and retreated to my room.

???

My brother, Mike, had graduated from high school in June, then spent the summer figuring out what he wanted to do with his life. After our ocean trip, he and Dad sat across from each other at Big Brick's blackened pine kitchen table. I lay on the couch in the family room, reading a Superman comic book.

"I'd like you to consider the military as a viable option," my father said with formal enunciation as he took a swig of scotch.

My siblings and I often laughed at how closely Drinking Dar resembled the character "Frederick" from an episode of *The Flintstones*. Fred Flintstone's entire personality had changed to a sophisticated gentleman after he was struck on the head by a bottle of Cactus Cola. He'd insisted on being called *Frederick* and his manner became sickeningly polite.

The likeness to my tipsy father was uncanny.

The reverse parallel fit just as snugly. In my father's sober moments, he resembled the everyday Fred, overweight, loud, easily irritated, sometimes fun.

Drinking Dar spoke to Mike. "The Air Force is a fine institution," he said. "You can receive an education without strapping a significant amount of debt to your shoulders."

The conversation hung there. I stopped reading, waiting for my brother's reply.

"Okay, I'll check it out," he said finally.

Through the open counter area that separated the two rooms I saw Dad smile. "They teach discipline. There comes a time in a young man's career when a little discipline will provide some solid footing," Drinking Dar continued.

I watched my brother, his face unreadable, listening as our father rambled on about the merits of the United States Armed Forces.

The next day, Mike talked to the Air Force recruiter in Arcadia. He came home with a handful of signed paperwork. They wanted him in Virginia at the beginning of September.

Three weeks later, we lay in the darkness, the last night Mike and I would share a room.

"Go to college, if you can," he said abruptly, as I drifted toward sleep.

"Okay," I said, shocked awake. We didn't say any more.

I turned over and tried to settle down, my mind whirling that he had shared something so grown up with me.

???

October arrived, painting the forest beyond the corn patch and the sugar maple in the front yard with vibrant reds and yellows. Winter was coming.

At Big Brick, I had to be out of bed by six thirty to guarantee I'd be on time for my bus' arrival. My morning rush to shower, dress, and eat grew increasingly dark and cold.

As the days shortened and autumn temperatures settled over Western New York, I found myself at the end of the driveway closer and closer to the seven thirty deadline. Around Thanksgiving, an early snow fell. The west wind howled across the top of our hill, piling drifts in the driveway.

Despite the colder weather, I sweated during my sprint down the driveway, trying to arrive before Merk chugged up the hill.

Jackie Merkum, my new bus driver, lived in the trailer park across from Gerard's Grocery. She shopped in our store frequently, always laughing a loud laugh and voicing strong opinions on any subject. I liked her most of the time – except whenever she mentioned that I should exercise more and lose some weight.

Unknown to our customers, Paul and I had made a game of assigning code names to many of them. There was *Cough*, the cigar-smoking chemical technician who hacked out his words like he had a fur ball stuck in his throat. *Lab Coat*, the hospital aide who stopped in for potato chips and candy bars before his evening shift. And *Gee's*, a nickname for the store itself.

Merk, a short, quick variation on her last name, seemed appropriate for Jackie. She was friendly sometimes, abrupt like my dad other times, and didn't believe in waiting around for kids – if you were *at* the bus stop, you *got* a ride.

The miss was inevitable, yet the day it happened, I was unprepared. One early December morning, I frantically searched for my coat in the library closet. The dozens of jackets that crammed the space thwarted my efforts. Mom discovered me on her way to prepare the Opes' breakfast. She sensed my distress.

"I'll go watch for the bus," she said. My mother opened the front door and stood, her slippers sticking to the thick crust of frost that had formed on the threshold. *Jupiter would remember where his coat was,* I thought. *Or he'd deduce its location.*

I gave up on the closet and ran upstairs. There was my jacket, piled on the floor in the corner of my bedroom. Mom yelled from the foyer. "She's *here*, Honey!" She waved her arms as I raced down the stairs, skipping every other one.

Big Brick sat way back from the road. The driveway twisted and curled for over a hundred feet before it met the top of the hill. I catapulted through the front door, only to see a flash of school-bus yellow roll by. I ground to a halt, my breath making rapid, puffy clouds in front of my face.

"She didn't even stop." Mom's tone sounded tight. "Go see if Paul can drive you to school on his way to the store."

Back upstairs, I pounded on the bathroom door. I heard the shower running.

"Paul! I missed the bus!" I yelled through the wood. "Mom wants you to drive me to school!"

"What'd you say?"

I drew a deep breath. "I MISSED THE BUS CAN YOU DRIVE ME TO SCHOOL?"

"Ummm, okay, but we're going to breakfast then. There's a new Perkins opening in Arcadia today."

"OKAY WITH ME!"

I headed back downstairs and plopped onto the couch, my armpits already damp through my golf-knit shirt. "He'll take me," I told my mom.

Paul appeared twenty minutes later and we piled into his car. My brother and I were no strangers to Perkins – a chain diner that had cropped up all over the area. We'd eaten there many times.

Arriving at the restaurant, I ordered in a rush, choosing my favorite pile of ham on a toasted bun – the Big Fritz. I loved to mix the sweetness of a Danish pastry with the saltiness of the ham. My Gerard's Grocery snack combination in different form. Paul ordered his regular omelet.

Wolfing down my food, I fiddled with the cream packets, waiting for my brother to finish. "I gotta be there by nine!" I said, when he ordered a third refill of coffee.

"Okay, okay." He took a long last swig. "But if we do this again, let's leave earlier."

I made it to school before the bell rang.

"Where were you?" Adam asked me in the schoolyard. "I didn't see you get off the bus."

"Paul drove me," I said, dropping my tone a notch. "We went out to breakfast."

Missing the bus quickly became a regular event. I enjoyed the door-to-door car ride – and breakfast with my brother. On the way, we talked about lots of things. Church, school, friends, Gerard's Grocery customers. He seemed happy to have the company and I liked that he listened to anything I had to say.

Back on the bus, Merk seemed put off by my new routine. "A Big Fritz!" she barked, when I told her what I ate at Perkins. "You'll never lose weight eating ham sandwiches for breakfast. Now me, I've started taking karate lessons with my boyfriend. It's great exercise and discipline. That's what you need, not going to Perkins everyday with Paul."

My detective skills couldn't sense whether she was mad about my being overweight or whether she resented that I didn't need to rely on her to get to school. Regardless of the motivation, I caught the self-satisfied twist of her lips in the bus-driver-is-watching-you mirror and decided not to argue the point.

???

Gerard's Grocery became fertile ground for me to hone my detective skills. Dad had just arrived home on a Sunday evening when we got a call from the local sheriff. The store alarm was blaring; a neighbor had reported it.

Dad and I piled into our Ford station wagon and cut through the snow that had drifted across the driveway. I brought my Lifesavers bag – the duffel I'd obtained by mailing in ten Lifesavers wrappers and five dollars.

I kept it packed with all the standard gear an investigator would need:

- ✓ a pen and my journal, for recording pertinent information
- ✓ a small mirror, for seeing around corners
- ✓ a piece of colored chalk, to mark my trail with the Three Investigators' triple-question-mark symbol: ???
- ✓ a Swiss pocketknife, to cut through bonds
- ✓ a camera and flash

All the equipment Jupiter used in the books.

Adding a tape measure to help document the crime scene, I was ready for action.

"It's probably a false alarm," Dad figured. "Maybe the wind rattled the back door. But I suppose we better check it out."

I gripped my journal in my left hand. When we reached the store, I wrote down the time: *7:53 p.m.*

A police cruiser sat in the parking lot, its exhaust visible in the chilly night air. Dad pulled up to the officer's car and rolled down the window. "You got hit, Darwin," the first one said.

81

My father's jaw fell open. I craned my neck to hear every word the cop said.

"Looks like they used a sledge hammer to smash the front door. I don't know if they got away with much, you might wanna take a look. There's some footprints here in the snow where they ran to a car parked off the road." He pointed past the ice-covered pond to a dark stretch of road. I slipped out of the car, desperate to see the damage.

"Goddamn it!" Dad shouted as he surveyed the shattered remains of the front door scattered down the main aisle. Small pieces of glass winked at us from beneath the chip rack. "You know how much that door glass costs?"

"You're insured, right?" one of the younger cops asked.

"Yeah, but this is a helluva mess." Dad stepped across the glass, crunching his way toward the register. I knew we didn't leave cash in the drawer, but my father kept rolled coin stored under the counter. Maybe fifty or sixty dollars worth. And, as part of the closing procedure, we always placed a small bag of starter cash for the morning shift in the freezer behind the counter.

The coin was gone. The frozen cash was safe.

"They probably had a hard time getting outta here with all that rolled coin in their pockets and the alarm screamin' in their ears." Dad smiled for the first time since we'd received the call.

A second squad car with two more policemen pulled up. Dad recognized one of them, a guy named Fred who lived in the neighborhood and shopped at Gerard's Grocery regularly. Paul and I called him *Ready Freddy* for his helpful-but-anxious manner. "Thanks for coming out, Fred," my father greeted him.

"What a damn shame, Dar!" Fred replied, pacing back and forth around the broken glass. "A *damn* shame!"

"I'm gonna look around outside," I said.

My breath hung in tiny clouds as I surveyed the parking lot. The tracks in the snow near the door were messed up by the cops, but I could see one clear set of prints heading toward the pond. Beyond that, tread marks cut through the frozen slush. Just like something from The Three Investigators.

I opened the Lifesavers bag and grabbed my camera and flash. I snapped a few pictures of the tire tracks, then moved to the shoe impressions.

Squatting over one of the clearest footprints, I took a few shots from different angles. I pulled out my notebook and drew a sketch of the pattern. Nancy Drew had done the same once – and it helped capture the criminal.

Pulling out the tape measure, I recorded the length and width of the print in my journal. Satisfied I had all the immediate details, I returned to the store.

Ready Freddy helped Dad put a piece of plywood over the hole in the empty door frame. I wondered whether I should show my notes to the police. Like Merk, I knew Fred pretty well; he shopped at our store almost every day.

Standing in the frigid air, watching them work to cover the door, I decided to keep my investigation private. I didn't want to risk them laughing at me. When the place was secure, Dad and I climbed back into the Ford and headed home.

On TV, crooks often returned to the scene of the crime. Over the next couple of weeks, I studied my sketches and watched customers come and go. I looked at all of their shoes, but there wasn't an easy way to measure size. And all of their tire tracks looked the same in Gee's muddy parking lot.

Frustrated, I packed my journal back into my nightstand drawer, wondering when I'd uncover a mystery that I could really sink my detective teeth into.

RUNAWAY PLAN: Cincinnati/Days Thirteen—Fourteen (1984)

The day for college approached. The night before I had to report, I picked up a twenty-pack of chicken nuggets and devoured them on my bedroom couch. The anxious tension in my stomach receded.

My freshman orientation at Xavier began the next morning. I parked Bufford in the visitor lot. Hand-made signs directed me to tables near the chapel, where I was assigned to join a small group of kids.

"Hi!" a girl with a deep, sassy voice greeted us. Red hair swirled around her face, reaching down to her shoulders. Like Nancy Drew, *I thought to myself.*

"Now there's a bunch of rules we have to cover, but guys, just hang with me, we'll get through this, and then we can talk about the good stuff, like parties off campus."

There were six of us in total: the red-haired girl, another blonde, and three guys. I tried to focus on remembering everyone, but as we met many more teachers and students in the throngs of people, I lost all track of names. For the first time, my Jupiter-detective skills abandoned me.

The day after Xavier orientation, I cruised around Cincinnati getting to know the street layout, then returned to the apartment. I had eaten lunch, but still felt hungry.

My sister, Molly, and I had finished off all of our munchies, so I made a quick trip to the grocery store. Passing the Park at Your Own Risk *sign on my return, I spotted Danny, our upstairs neighbor, walking his dog, Chauncey. A girl strolled along with them. As I unpacked Bufford, they approached.*

"Greg, this is my girlfriend, Liz," Danny said.

She and I both spoke at the same time. "Hi."

I smiled and made small talk for a few minutes. When they continued on their walk, I watched, feeling a sense of rejection inside my belly that I knew wasn't rational.

I sat down in Bufford's front seat. Tears bubbled up from nowhere. I blinked hard*, willing them away. I tried to laugh, to discharge the feelings that were surfacing, but my regular emotional release – hysterical cackling – escaped me. I sat in the heat of the late summer afternoon and talked to myself.*

So he isn't gay.

So what?

What would you have done if he was?

I finally locked the car and entered the building. It was a long walk up the four flights, my head feeling as heavy as the grocery bags I carried. When I reached the apartment, I immediately broke out the pretzel rods, M&Ms, and 7-UP.

Chapter Six: Superman (1979)

Tuesday, February 27, 1979

I have been having very conflicting thoughts. I thought a year ago that I would be a priest for sure. But now I kind of want to make it with a girl and have a bunch of kids.

MIKE WENT OUT with girls all the time. Even Paul, with all his health problems, had been to the prom. I was reminded of this every time I dragged the projector out of Big Brick's attic and ran the family slides.

At twelve, I sensed I was expected to do the same, by Mike, by my friends, by everybody. That's what guys did – at least until they entered the priesthood. *Then it won't matter.*

Gaila and I had become friends during a Saint Mike's student council rally. I liked her kooky laugh and the way her thick brown hair cascaded over her shoulders. If I *had* to go on a date, she seemed like a good choice.

Movies were for dates, everybody knew that. And I *really* wanted to see the new movie, Superman. The perfect match.

"What do you think?" I asked Adam in homeroom. He raised his eyebrows.

"You're gonna ask her on a date?" My best friend seemed surprised.

"Yeah, do you like her?" I pressed him.

He shrugged his shoulders and smiled. "She seems okay. Go for it, Cassanova!"

Riding this wave of confidence, I approached Gaila's desk at lunch. "Hey," I started, stepping too close in my haste. She moved away.

"Yeees?" she asked, pulling a strand of hair from between her braces.

"I was thinkin' about seeing the new Superman movie—" I trailed off.

"Gregory Gerard, are you asking me on a date?" she spoke too loudly. I looked around, but nobody seemed interested in our conversation.

"Yeah, that's what I was thinking."

She rolled her eyes and considered my request. "Well, I'll have to ask my mother, but it's probably okay," she said.

I forged ahead. "Great! Let's go this Sunday afternoon."

"Okay," she agreed.

I returned to my desk and breathed in short gasps, giving a "thumbs up" sign to Adam.

The following Sunday after Mass, Paul drove me to Gaila's house in Arcadia. I walked up to her door, trying to keep my hands from shaking. She answered the bell. "Hi."

"Hi." *This is just like being friends in school,* I told myself. My stomach disagreed.

"My mom wants to meet you," she said as an older, thinner version of Gaila appeared.

"Hello, Greg. It's nice to meet you. You take good care of my Gaila today."

"Awwwww, Mom!" Gaila whined.

"It's nice to meet you," I spoke up, anxious to get moving.

"Okay, okay, you be a good girl. Home by five thirty!" her mom instructed. She kissed Gaila and we piled into Paul's car. "Hello!" Gaila's mom waved to my brother.

Paul dumped us in front of the theater. I'd already instructed him to be back in exactly two hours. Our Perkins was right next door. *He'll probably sit there the whole time*, I thought. *Sipping coffee and talking to our regular waitress.*

I paid for the tickets, snacks, and drinks – thanks to an emergency stipend from the second-drawer down. Gaila thanked me and we settled into our seats just before the previews came on.

Was I supposed to put my arm around her? I clutched the large bin of popcorn to my chest to ensure my hands were busy.

That's rude. Guilt flushed over me in a wave. "You want some?" I thrust the snack toward her, spilling some in the process.

"Okay." She took a large handful. I perched the bin on my knee so we could both reach it. It twitched slightly with the trembling of my leg, but Gaila didn't seem to notice.

The movie started and I began to relax. Christopher Reeve *was* the Superman I'd envisioned from my comic books. I drank in his sturdy face, his powerful frame. Gaila sat forgotten for most of the film, except during the occasional interruption for more popcorn.

When the credits flashed across the screen, we stood to leave.

"Wasn't that *good*?" I asked her.

"Yeah," she agreed.

"The only thing I didn't like was that he broke the rule about interfering with time. That was the one thing he wasn't supposed to do."

She turned and yanked my arm. "He did it to save Lois!" she screeched louder than I'd expected. I glanced at the other patrons. A few kids looked our way, but nobody said anything.

"She was his girlfriend! She would have died otherwise!" Gaila continued, when I didn't respond.

I rushed her toward the exit, hoping Paul was waiting. I spied his Oldsmobile in the bright afternoon sun. "Well—I still don't like that he had to break the rules. Besides, why would turning the world backwards turn back time?" Adding some Jupiter-logic might calm her down.

"Arrrh!" Gaila made a wordless noise as I pushed her toward the car. This wasn't going as smoothly as I'd hoped.

I opened the car door and shifted the conversation away from Superman and Lois. "Paul, where'd you spend the two hours?"

"Perkins," he answered.

We climbed in and he pulled away from the curb. Gaila sat in the rider's seat, not speaking. My stomach, quelled with popcorn, began to gurgle, anticipating the next hurdle. Everything I'd ever heard about dates included a *goodnight kiss.*

It's only afternoon, I thought. *That doesn't qualify.*

I liked Gaila, but the thought of pressing my lips to hers made me feel as if a plastic garbage bag were over my head – while someone slowly tightened the pull string. I wanted out, as quickly as possible.

At her house, I walked her to the door.

Gaila spoke first. "Well, see ya. Thanks for the movie and popcorn. Even if you don't think it's worth breaking a rule to save your girlfriend!" she gave me one final jab. Her eyes darted from my face to the ground, then back to my face.

"I had fun, too. See ya in school!" I said.

And quickly retreated to the car.

Sunday, April 8, 1979

I went on my first date today with Gaila. We saw Superman. It was a great movie. I was really nervous before it, and after it I threw up.

P.S. I lost four pounds so far this month by dieting!

P.P.S. I got $60.00 saved already for Ocean City where Paul, Mike and I are going in August for a great beach vacay!

???

My oldest sister, Molly, had maintained a bedroom at Big Brick, but she'd spent much of her time away at nursing school. After graduation, she moved back in with us for a few months until she accepted a nurse's job at an adult care facility in Cincinnati. The night before she left, I wandered into her bedroom carrying a bag of Oreos. She was shoving clothes into a tall cardboard box.

"How will we stay in touch?" I asked, sprawling across her bed.

"Well, it's not that expensive to fly to Cincinnati and we can write anytime." I watched her seal the last box with transparent mailing tape, then she slumped onto the bed beside me. We broke into the Oreos together, plowing through them.

I looked up, noticing that dead flies had gathered inside the ceiling's light fixture. We had them in every bedroom of Big Brick: flies trapped between bulb and diffuser. Piles of insects that'd silently suffocated.

I split a cookie in half and scraped the white goo into my mouth with my front teeth. "So you're gonna work with Opes?" I asked.

"Yeah," she laughed. "Just like home."

I watched my sister carefully. "What's it feel like, to be going so far away from home?" I asked.

Molly stared at the ceiling. "I don't know. It'll be different, I guess. Sorta like living at nursing school, but just a more expensive phone call."

My big sister paused, then laughed again. "What if I end up paying more money for the phone bill than my apartment?" We both giggled, then laughed, then howled. Our laughing fit continued for some time as a dull pain settled into my gut, both from the hard laughing and from all the cookies I'd eaten. Tears trickled out of my eyes, blurring the image of tiny fly corpses caught in the fixture above my head.

???

Paul and I continued the Perkins trips throughout the school year. We always found plenty to talk about during the ride. "Sing the Saint Michael's song again," Paul said as we rode toward our restaurant.

I'd learned the words from Adam at school, later singing it around Big Brick. Paul had laughed out loud. I launched into the familiar lyrics:

Give a cheer, give a cheer
For the boys who make the beer,
In the cellar of Saint Michael's School.

91

Oh I hope that they don't find
That we're down here all the time
In the cellar of Saint Michael's School.

Run! Run! Run!
I think I hear a nun.
Grab all the liquor you can hold.
If she grabs you by the ear
Say, 'Sister, have a beer!'
In the cellar of Saint Michael's School.

Paul chuckled. "That song cracks me up," he said, pulling into Perkins' parking lot. I couldn't believe that he, the most Catholic of us all – who wouldn't even tell a little white lie if Mom asked him to – enjoyed the song about beer in the basement of Saint Mike's.

Merk continued to give me flack for eating a Big Fritz at breakfast. "That's why you put on a spare tire," she explained, staring at my bottom as I walked down the bus aisle. "I'm tellin' ya, karate is the way to go, it's great exercise! And I should know; I'm getting to be a regular expert, heh heh heh!"

My cheeks burned with her loud words. She reminded me of my dad; when he raised his voice, he said whatever he felt, regardless of who was listening. For once, I felt relieved that I lived so far away from Saint Mike's. I was one of the first kids on the bus. Not many other kids were present to witness Merk's assessment of my "spare tire."

Finding a seat near the back, I vowed to ride to school with Paul more frequently.

???

I began to long for a functional detective agency. I wanted a place I could model after The Three Investigators.

By now I'd read almost all of their stories, including my favorites: *The Mystery of the Screaming Clock*, *The Mystery of the Fiery Eye*. I idolized Jupiter's ability to outthink the crooks, even if he ate too much. Nancy Drew, Frank and Joe Hardy were all thin, attractive, and athletic – everybody expected them to succeed.

In the books, Jupiter created a headquarters in a used trailer, hidden behind junk in his uncle's salvage yard. Headquarters was stocked with everything: phone, photo lab, secret entrances. Just the kind of place I needed.

Adam rode the bus home with me on a Friday night and we discussed the problem. After dinner, we searched all around Big Brick.

I thought of the grain bin, the one my brother, Mike, had shown me, the place I'd read the *Playboy*. It was hard to get to, dark, and dank – but very well hidden. Adam and I climbed to the second floor of the barn to consider the possibility.

We ascended the creaky stairs. I hooked the flashlight I'd brought into my belt, crossed the stage, and climbed the ladder over the half-wall on the far side. Adam peeked his head over the edge of the wall. "This is so cool!" he said.

Similar to my previous visits, darkness clouded my view, with only the flashlight and an indirect glow filtering down from the small window high above. One after the other, we climbed down the interior ladder. Small clouds of dust rose like mini-tornadoes in the flashlight's beam. I began a sneezing fit as Adam reached my side.

"This is perfect," he said.

"As soon as we clean it up and get some more light in here."

In the center of the floor, I found a vent hole. "This is probably to send grain down to the first floor for the cows." I tried to sound sure, as I imagined Jupiter would be. I pushed it open and peered through. The hole was about six by six inches, large enough to pass evidence through, if we were attacked from above.

I stood up and surveyed the rest of the room. In contrast to the inch of grime on the floor, the walls appeared clean. The slotted boards formed a tight fit, probably to keep the grain from spilling out the sides. I liked that our secrets would be contained as easily as the grain had been.

"Now *this* is a Headquarters," I said, very pleased. Adam shook his head in agreement.

We spent the rest of the evening sweeping grime through the vent hole into a large garbage can.

The next morning, we carried a few boards up from the first floor, which we laid across the top of the bin, creating a ceiling. That was all we could do before Paul took Adam home. "I can come back next weekend," my friend told me as he left.

"Great. I'll work on it this week."

"'K. See ya, man."

"Not if I see you first," I said, waving as Paul's Oldsmobile pulled away.

I stayed in the barn all day, cleaning and sneezing. Near suppertime, I completed the final task: snaking an extension cord to power Headquarters out of sight behind the barn rafters.

In a household full of siblings, Opes – and any number of enemies once my detective efforts became renowned – I was determined to keep my use of the grain bin as HQ a secret known only to me, Adam, and my detective's journal.

Tuesday May 15, 1979
Adam and I started to build a Three Investigators Headquarters in the barn this weekend. I bought great walkie-talkies today for our cases.

Over the next week, I worked late into the evenings, setting up a workbench, a desk area, a hot plate, and a fluorescent clock I commandeered from the piles of stuff on the first floor. I bought a used CB radio from a kid on the bus and installed it above the workbench.

I stocked a small shelf with a box of Nestle Crunch bars and a canister of dried Lipton soup packets – compliments of Gerard's

Grocery. They seemed like good sustenance, in case I was ever trapped in HQ for an extended period of time.

My portable radio got good reception inside Headquarters. Turning through the AM dial one night, I discovered a program that was perfect to build a detective agency by. *The CBS Radio Mystery Theater*, a one-hour mystery drama, was broadcast each night at ten o'clock. I loved the creaking door that opened the show and the host's, E.G. Marshall's, case-like introduction to each episode. I began spending every night in my new headquarters listening to the show as I organized my office.

"What are you doing out there?" Paul asked. He couldn't understand why I suddenly chose to stay in the barn so late at night, but I wasn't ready to reveal my secret.

"Just hanging out," I said, cringing at the weakness of my excuse.

???

I could tell my brother, Mike, was lonely in the Air Force. He wrote me weekly letters as our Ocean City trip drew closer. We talked more on paper than we ever had in person.

He worked in the cryptography section of the Force. One week he sent me a stack of brain teasers. I attacked them with enthusiasm, believing that Jupiter would be able to solve them. I sealed my results and mailed them to Virginia. He replied with the answers the following week. I opened the envelope from the stack of mail and scanned the pages. I'd gotten some of them right, but I wasn't sure if it was enough to impress him.

???

Mom and Dad invited a bunch of people to our house for a summer party. While my mother and sisters stacked shaved ham and pre-cut rolls onto a long table in the dining room, my father set up his electric piano on Big Brick's front porch.

One by one, guests began to arrive, including Caroline and her parents from across the street. A saxophone, a bass, and a drum set joined Dad's piano on the porch. The quartet began to play swing tunes. A few couples danced on our front sidewalk.

Dad had set up a bar in the kitchen, a long row of bottles on the jet-black counter. The scotch, vodka, and gin bottles were all newly purchased. Caroline and I watched the adults approach and fill their glasses.

"It's a helluva party, Betty!" Caroline's dad yelled to my mother across the kitchen, ice cubes tinkling in his glass.

"I want to try a drink," I whispered to my friend. Her face twisted as though she'd sucked on one of the lemon wedges that peppered Big Brick's counter.

"You're too young!" she insisted. She was only ten, but I was thirteen. *Old enough*, I thought.

"I'm gonna ask my mom," I said, determined to try. I approached my mother, who piled dishes into the sink. A woman stood at her left, talking and smoking.

I tugged at the sleeve of Mom's dress. "Is it okay if I have a drink?" I said.

She glanced toward me. "Sure, Honey," she said, then continued her conversation with the lady-guest.

I suspected she didn't know I meant alcohol, but my Catholic conscience felt relieved that I'd asked permission. There'd be nothing to report to Father McFarland in the confessional.

I grabbed a plastic glass and filled it with orange juice. Pausing casually, I tipped the vodka bottle toward my glass. An inch of clear fluid mixed with my OJ. Nobody but Caroline saw it.

My friend and I went out to the front yard as I gulped down the orange mixture in the hot afternoon sun. It tasted slightly bitter.

After several minutes, my head began to feel light and airy. I giggled. The band kicked off a raucous melody.

"Let's dance. I think this music is called Dixieland," I said to Caroline.

She followed me onto the far side of the wrap-around porch, out of sight of the performers. We linked arms and ran in circles, kicking up our heels, as I'd seen people do on TV. My whole body felt as light as a butterfly hovering over the field grass next to the house.

"I like drinking!" I yelled to my ten-year old friend.

She kept dancing, but a dark furrow cut across her forehead.

???

June 27, 1979

I am trying to become a Jupiter. I am taking the walkie-talkie apart to see how it works. It's really interesting.

Adam and I have got the greatest secret Headquarters up in the grain bin on the second floor of the barn!

First Investigator, Greg

PS. I can hardly wait for August 3 -18, 1979. Mike, Paul and I are going to Ocean City! Yahoo!

Headquarters had surpassed my initial plans, but I continued to make improvements. In The Three Investigators, the boys had a couple of entrances to thwart enemies. I used a circular saw to cut a small hole in the floor and added a hinged cover. It opened just above some stored furniture. I could step down onto it, scramble onto the workbench, and jump to the floor. I now had an escape hatch. I called it Tunnel Two, mimicking Jupiter Jones' second entrance.

My dad got a new alarm system at the store. I saw him pack the old siren into a box in the backroom. "Can I have this?" I asked, trying to avoid any questions.

"Go ahead," he said, distracted by an argument he was having with the beer salesman.

I brought it home and installed it just above HQ's ceiling. Because we'd done so much renovation on Big Brick, there were always boxes of leftover electrical equipment lying around the barn. I found a few light switches and brought them up. I cut up an extension cord and ran it from a control panel I'd fashioned to the siren above. Everything was in place.

I flipped the switch I'd marked *Siren*. The wail echoed through the cavernous space of the second floor as pigeons flapped madly about. I switched it off.

"Cool," I said out loud, munching on one of the Hershey's almond bars I'd brought from Gee's to replace the box of Nestle Crunch, which I'd already finished.

<h2 style="text-align:center">???</h2>

My sister, Kathy, scheduled a clothing trip to the mall. I opted to join her, to look over the latest technology at Radio Shack. I might find something for use in my detective agency.

Inside the store, I spotted a telephone intercom system. I checked the price, $13.95. In my wallet I had a twenty dollar bill I'd taken from Mom's second-drawer down. *What could I use the phones for?* An idea popped into my head. Sold.

That evening, I unwound the cable that ran between the two units. *Fifty feet*, the directions stated. Enough to reach from Paul's bedroom to mine. I set up my phone on the floor next to my bed and ran the gray-blue wire along the carpet's edge in the hallway. I looped it around Paul's doorframe, setting his phone on the headboard of his bed.

"Let's try it out," he said enthusiastically.

I.beeped from my room; he picked up almost immediately.

" 'Nello," Paul said. "Have I reached the party to whom I am speaking?"

"It is I." I tried to speak like Jupiter would.

"This is pretty cool."

"Yeah and we don't have to pay long distance!" I joked.

"Not unless Ma Bell hears about this."

We talked late into the night about our upcoming vacation, customers, Saint Michael's, whatever came into our heads.

The week of our Ocean City trip, I packed my book bag with the necessities – beach towel, sun glasses, comic books. I was missing sun tan lotion. Paul kept several bottles on his dresser – he loved the sunshine. I walked down the hall.

My brother lay on his bed fully clothed, pressing an ice pack against the indentation in his skull. The spitty basin rested on the floor nearby.

"What's the matter with you?" I asked.

"I got a headache," he said, his right eye focusing on me while the left gazed into space, like it sometimes did when he had head pressure.

I rested my hand on his headboard. "Well, do you need anything?"

"Nahh. Mom just wants me to rest. She's calling the doctor."

I grabbed a bottle of Coppertone off his dresser. "Can I borrow this for O.C.?"

He focused on the bottle for a moment, then closed both eyes. "Sure."

Tuesday, August 7, 1979
We are not going to Ocean City. Paul is sick, he has to have brain surgery tomorrow.

Mom walked out of the house behind me. We were going to the hospital for Paul's operation. Everybody else would be along in a minute.

"Honey," she said, putting her arm around me. "You know that he might not make it through the surgery."

"*I know*," I said, emphasizing the words, feeling heat rise in my cheeks. *Did she think I didn't know such a simple thing?*

"Okay, Honey. You two have become such pals this past year, I wanted to make sure you knew how serious this is." Dad, Anne, and Kathy joined us and we piled into our massive station wagon.

In the hospital waiting room, I wavered between clinical Jupiter detachment and fervent praying. "Jesus, please let my brother be okay," I pleaded.

August 10, 1979

Paul's surgery was a success. The upper part of his shunt was clogged with protein tissue.

P.S. I have to go back to school soon. Yuck!

Paul came home from the hospital after a few days, but he wasn't able to return to the store for awhile. We all put in extra shifts to help out. At home, I introduced him to *The CBS Radio Mystery Theater*. It quickly became our nighttime routine: to listen to the program and eat bowls of ice cream together.

Each Sunday at Saint Pat's, they mentioned my brother's name as part of the community prayer list. People approached us after Mass, asking how he was doing.

"Oh, he's coming along," Mom said to all of them.

Paul and I chatted on our bedroom phones while I packed my book bag for the first day of eighth grade – my last year at Saint Michael's.

"Does your head hurt?" I asked him.

"Nahhh, I just hope my hair doesn't give up the ghost. I don't have any to spare." I laughed. Same old Paul. "They said my old shunt was clogged with protein."

"Yeah, I heard. How long is a shunt supposed to last?"

He thought for a minute. "Well, they did the last surgery in '76 and that's only three years. But they tell me I should be good for another ten."

"You'll be thirty seven before you need one again!"

"That's what they tell me."

My finger slipped and hit the button that signaled Paul's phone. A loud beep stung both our ears.

"Youch!" he said through the receiver.

"Sorry, that was me."

"Alll-righty. That oughta clear out any protein left in my head."

I chuckled again. "Well, just work on getting better 'cause I think I might be missing the bus sometime soon."

"I'll work on it," he promised.

The next day was blazing for September. I stood at the end of the driveway early. Merk pulled up, the brakes screeching as she slowed to a stop. "How's Paul doing?" she asked when the doors popped open. The customers missed him as much as the parishioners.

"He's getting better. He can't work at the store for awhile, though."

"No Big Fritz anytime soon, huh?"

"No," I said as she closed the doors and ground the gears. As I took my seat, I searched the mirror to see if she seemed pleased, but her face only registered concern.

Arrival at school seemed different this year. We were the *eighth* graders, the oldest kids on the property. It felt powerful.

I was happy to see Adam again. "Hello, Gregor," he said as we settled into homeroom.

"Hello, Adaman," I replied. "Did you watch *Bionic Woman* last week?"

"Of course." We discussed the episode as the school year got under way.

Friday, September 21, 1979
Paul has had a relapse. He went to the hospital. He will be operated on Monday.

It started in the usual way. Paul got more headaches and threw up, the same as he had in August. Mom couldn't believe it.

"Oh my God, Darwin," she said to Dad when he got home from the store. Her voice was trembly, like it sounded when the furnace made funny noises or a water pipe leaked. "Do you think it's his shunt?"

Dad studied Paul, whose bumpy skull shined in the harsh light from the nightstand lamp. "Now just slow down, Mom. Let's take this one step at a time."

He moved closer to look into Paul's eyes, accidentally kicking into the spitty basin. I grabbed it and moved it away.

Paul said nothing, rubbing the depression in his head, the same spot he'd used to pump away the pain when he was seven.

It was swollen.

My father finally spoke. "I guess we better ship him back up to the hospital."

"Oh my God," Mom shuddered in the background.

Dad and Mom drove Paul to Strong Hospital the next day. Another CAT scan revealed more pressure in Paul's head. "We'll do surgery Monday morning," the doctors told my parents.

Two surgeries in two months felt more critical than usual — and the family responded. Molly arranged to fly home the next day from Cincinnati and Mike said he would hitch a ride up from Virginia.

"Sorta like a Walton's operation," Kathy joked as we got into the car Monday morning. I skipped school at The Booker's request. Mom had trouble covering the Old People and the store on such short notice, so we all helped.

My sister dropped me at Gerard's Grocery to cover the day shift, then she drove home to watch the Opes.

I set out my M&Ms, pretzels, and 7-UP. For once, I was a grateful to be busy with customers. It made the time pass more quickly.

Anne showed up to relieve me around three.

"Is there any word yet?" I asked.

"No. But it doesn't mean anything bad, he could just be in post-op for a long time." A budding nurse herself, Anne always knew facts like that.

At home that night, Kathy and I served the Opes' supper, then waited. The phone rang around eight.

Kathy got to it first. "Hello?" she spoke into the receiver. "Yeah." Pause. "Yeah." More pause.

"Is he okay?" I whispered at her. She covered the mouthpiece.

"Yeah, hold on," she mouthed at me. I paced the kitchen for a minute, then headed for the ice cream freezer while she continued to talk. Finally, she hung up.

"So what's the story?" I asked as I pulled out the vanilla ice cream, then scrounged in the cupboard for chocolate sauce and Spanish peanuts.

"He had to have another pump put in. I guess the first one wasn't working right. They left them both in. But he's doing okay."

"Are Mom, Dad, Mike, and Molly comin' right home?"

"They're gonna stop for dinner somewhere, then be home later."

"You want some ice cream?"

Kathy looked at me, her dainty white collar poking out from beneath a matching sweater.

"Okay, but I gotta call Anne to tell her Paul's all right."

"I'll wait for ya," I said, pulling another bowl down from the cupboard.

Paul came home a few days later and everybody returned to their normal routine. His second recovery went much like the first. He spent the majority of his time in bed, reading and sleeping. We talked every night on our Radio Shack phones.

"What's it like to have brain surgery?" I asked.

"Oh, I don't know. Same as any other surgery, I guess. Except you come out bald afterwards."

I giggled.

By the time Paul's hair had grown into a crisp crew cut, he was ready to return to the store. I noticed that he had more trouble remembering things.

Mom still relied on him to pull up odd facts from the past – things like *Bessie Heckman*, the name of an old lady who helped her care for Kathy, Mike, and Anne when they were babies. Recent memories confounded him, like remembering to bring home milk from the store when we called and placed an order. He stubbornly refused to write anything down.

???

The phone system for teachers at Saint Michael's consisted of a hockey-puck shaped receiver attached to a slotted metal wall grate. During English class, it beeped twice. My eighth-grade English and Religion teacher, Sister Emily, a gray-haired woman with an air of holiness about her gentle movements, approached, lifted the receiver, and spoke into the grate.

"Yes?"

She listened for a moment, then her eyes darted to me.

My stomach knotted.

"Okay, thank you, Sister." The teacher hung up and turned to face the class. "Greg, Sister Joyce would like you to stop down to the principal's office. Your father is here."

The noose on my gut tightened a notch. I had *never* been summoned to her office before. *Why was my dad here? Did something happen to Paul?*

The rest of the students began to moan with mock seriousness.

"That's enough," Sister Emily admonished them.

"Whatdja do?" Adam said. I shrugged, standing from beneath my desk.

Sister Emily smiled at me. "You're excused."

I walked the length of the eighth-grade wing, not rushing. Down the stairs, I turned the corner into the principal's office. My father's girth filled the chair across from Sister Joyce.

"Hi, Greg," he said. "I had some business in the area, so I thought I'd stop in and see what it is you do here."

"Take a seat," Sister Joyce indicated a second chair. I sat, my own hips tight between the arm rests. I wondered where this was headed.

"I was just telling your father how pleased we are with your performance here, Greg. Your grades are the highest in your class."

My stomach unclenched. We were on smooth ground. "Mr. Gerard, have you considered continuing Greg's Catholic education into high school?"

"My wife and I have considered the possibility, but the options are limited in Pal-Mac." I looked at my father, surprised. His tone had taken on its *proper* inflection – without the alcohol. I'd never heard Drinking Dar emerge without the encouragement of scotch whiskey.

I tilted my head slightly toward my principal and pinched my lower lip, attempting to look studious. *As Jupiter would.*

Sister leaned toward us, smiling widely. "Have you considered McQuaid Jesuit up in Rochester? My brothers attended McQuaid and they have wonderful things to say about it."

"That's a possibility," Dad crunched his brow. "Of course, expense is a consideration. He's The Caboose and a couple of the brood are still under our roof." Now he sounded more like my regular dad.

Sister Joyce nodded. "I feel that Greg would benefit from McQuaid. It's a college-preparatory institution and, considering Greg's grades, he would have no problem passing the entrance exam. The fact that they only accept boys provides a certain *focus* on education that other schools might not have."

My father chuckled. Sister Joyce's grin broadened.

"Of course, they emphasize the same Catholic character building and morals that we do here at Saint Michael's." She turned to me. "I think you would love it," she said. "What do you think, Greg?"

My cheeks felt hot, basking in the praise my principal had given me in front of my father. I liked the idea of an exclusive school in the city.

"It sounds great!"

My father spoke up. "Sister, your recommendation speaks very highly to me. Mrs. Gerard and I will discuss it." Drinking Dar again.

He's being formal because she's a nun, I thought.

She sat back, pulling out a pad and pen. "With your permission, I'll get in touch with the appropriate people at McQuaid and have them send you more information."

"Please do. Thank you, Sister. We've always thought very highly of Saint Michael's."

She scribbled a note on the pad. "And we think very highly of Greg."

I casually touched the back of my hand to my face. It didn't feel warm on the outside – which surprised me. It burned inside.

"Now, you'd better head back to English, young man," she excused me. We all stood. She extended her hand to my father. "It was a pleasure to see you again, Mr. Gerard."

He clasped her hand and shook succinctly. "We're always happy to hear good news about this one," he tipped his head at me, smiling. "That's all we ever seem to hear."

"That seems to be all we have to say about him," I heard her say. My thoughts were already elsewhere. *An all-boy school in the city. Wow.*

???

The tingling below my belt had increased since my escapades at the pool with Adam. More frequently I woke with an anxious swelling in my groin, enjoying the pressure of my body against the mattress. Something was going on down there. I wasn't sure what exactly it was – but it felt *good*.

I stepped into my homeroom's coat closet a few weeks after Dad visited Sister Joyce. Adam and a few of our friends huddled, speaking in low tones. I joined the tight circle.

"Yeah, Melody's boobs are really filling out," one of them said about a girl in our class.

"She shouldn'ta started wearing a bra. Did you see it through her blouse? Things were just starting to get interesting."

They laughed in unison and I joined in, although Melody's chest and her new bra-wearing habits hadn't caught my observant detective's eye. They went on to talk about another girl's physical attributes.

I enjoyed huddling with my friends, feeling their passion. And their physical closeness.

October 7, 1979

I can't believe it. I was sitting in the tub, and I was spraying water on my dick and really getting my thrills and all of the sudden I feel like I'm gonna pee and some white stuff is coming out. I had an ejaculation. This is the time and date: 6:10PM, October 7, 1979. It feels like I dreamt it all. But I know I didn't. Right now, I feel drained, secure and manly.

What I didn't choose to record was that, the whole time I'd been in the bathtub, I hadn't been thinking about Gaila, or Melody, or even Nancy Drew.

I'd been thinking about Superman.

RUNAWAY PLAN: Cincinnati/Weeks Three—Four (1984)

Two days after orientation, college classes began. Chemistry, Calculus, French, Basic Programming. I had a full schedule. As a commuter, I received a sticker for Bufford's window and directions to a vast student parking lot, far from the row of brick classrooms.

Rain pelted my car as I pulled in on the first day. The morning had slipped past faster than expected – I might not make it to class on time.

The empty spots were at the furthest corner of the lot. I opened the car door as huge droplets of water slapped against my arm. I pulled back, searching for something to cover me. I didn't own an umbrella.

Back home in Pal-Mac, the farthest I'd had to park from any building was a short dash. Rain gear had never been a staple in my wardrobe. Bucking up, I hoisted my book bag over my head and jogged through the torrent. I arrived at my first class, Chemistry, soaking wet and gasping for breath.

"Take an open seat," the professor commanded. I didn't need to be Jupiter to read the disdain dripping from his tone as liberally as the rainwater dribbled off my hair. He passed me a thin packet of papers. I shoved them into my textbook and sat down, feeling tiny rivulets of water run down my legs.

Over the first couple of weeks of school, I struggled to catch the routine of college. School had always come easily to me, but Xavier was different. I was different, off kilter, more than ever before. I'd somehow managed to belong before, at least on the outside.

I saw a poster on campus that Xavier had scheduled a welcoming Mass in the school's chapel at ten a.m. that coming Sunday. I hadn't been to church for several weeks, although I *hadn't stopped talking to God. I made a mental note of the time, vowing to return to my Catholic routine.*

The familiarity might help ground my thoughts, which fired and flared almost out of control. The same mystery – my grand secret – that I'd manage to contain over the years swirled through my head, threatening to split my life wide open.

Somehow, I just couldn't make it all fit inside me anymore.

Sunday arrived, but I didn't feel like going to Mass. Instead, I drove down to the river and watched the still water trundle by.

Chapter Seven: Covert Research (1979 continued)

WE'D HAD THE sex class with Mrs. Stirpe over a year ago, but it hadn't prepared me for the steamy excitement of October 7. By the following week, I had three similar experiences under my belt. The bathroom became my favorite room at Big Brick.

Father Fredricks stopped by our eighth-grade homeroom on a Tuesday afternoon. His unannounced visits to our Religion class were not uncommon, but today he greeted Sister Emily differently.

They didn't exchange words. Just a nod, as though executing a clandestine plan. Our teacher managed a quick exit, closing the door behind her.

We stood when he entered, as we had been taught. He motioned for us to sit, then turned to the chalkboard.

The priest retrieved a piece of white chalk from the tray and wrote two words on the board:

FORNICATION

MASTURBATION

A chill gripped my stomach. I wasn't clear on their meaning, but I knew they were bad words. No one blinked, shrugged, or breathed as he turned to face us.

"Children," he began, then paused. His gaze did not linger. He looked at our faces. At the floor. Over our heads.

Father Fredricks began again.

"Do you know what fornication is? That's when two people have relations before marriage."

I nodded quickly, anxious to be perceived as street-smart.

"And masturbation? That's when—"

He stopped speaking for a second time. His lips opened as though he were going to say more words, but nothing came out. Instead, he lifted his right hand in front of his face, turning it slowly back and forth in a presidential wave.

I knew what he was talking about. I had been in the bathtub.

He lowered his hand and continued. "There's a proper place for sexual relations. It is the sacramental covenant of marriage. That's where God intended these feelings to be expressed.

"The other behaviors, they are sins. God isn't pleased when we do them. Our bodies are temples of the Holy Spirit. When we fornicate or masturbate, we desecrate that temple."

Father Fredricks wrapped up his speech hurriedly, his gaze continuing to roam the room. He erased the board and left, returning to the sanctuary across South Main Street.

We sat whispering in huddled giggles until Sister Emily returned. She continued with our regular religion lesson as though Father Fredricks had never been there, but I could still make out the faint trace of the words on the front board: FORNICATION MASTURBATION.

The priest's speech had a profound effect on me. It did little to limit my visits to the bathtub, but along with the explosive pleasure came a new feeling.

Shame.

???

The time came for my next sibling to move out of Big Brick. My sister, Kathy, found an apartment in the city, rooming with a girl she knew from secretary college. Her new place was near Twelve Corners, an area where three major roads overlapped, forming a busy triangle of shops and services. We didn't have anything like that in Pal-Mac. Anne told me the place was also within walking distance of McQuaid Jesuit, the all-boy high school I might attend.

With Kathy gone, it would leave just Anne, Paul, Mom, Dad, me, and the Opes. Like Molly and Mike before, I would miss her around the house.

My thinnest sister spent some time packing. Her records. Her color-coordinated work outfits. Her stuffed animal collection. Where Molly's car had been crammed with nurse uniforms, books, and white sneakers, Kathy's had an orderly pile of cardboard boxes snuggled in the rear of her Pinto wagon.

Anne and I rode with her to help unload in the tiny city bedroom. "Wow!" I said, looking over the kitchen, the living room – and checking out the bathtub. "This is cool! When can I come visit?"

My sister's eyes grew shiny. "Whenever you want," she said.

???

Underneath the guilt about my bathtub activity, concern nagged at me. Although I'd been naive about the specifics of masturbation, I understood that boys should think about girls – breasts, specifically – while they did it.

My thoughts were always of boys.

To combat the unease tickling at my gut, I needed more information.

I'll solve this mystery like Jupiter would, I thought. Over the December holidays, I conducted covert research.

Beginning at the Macedon library, I walked up and down the aisles. "May I help you?" The librarian, an older woman with puffy cheeks smiled at me. A pair of half-glasses bounced against her chest, suspended by a gray band.

"No thanks, I'm just looking," I said. I grabbed a medium-sized tan book off the shelves. *God is My Co-Pilot* was stamped across the front. I shoved it under my arm and, maintaining my studious air, browsed casually toward the row marked "Sexuality."

I looked over my shoulder. No one in sight.

I paused and scanned the shelf. Of the many selections, one title caught my eye. *Human Sexuality*. My hand shook as I slid the

113

book from the shelf and rushed to the furthest corner of the library – behind the encyclopedias.

I held *God is My Co-Pilot* in my lap and placed *Human Sexuality* inside the larger book. I scanned the index, checking frequently to make sure no one approached.

Homosexuality had several listings.

I turned to the referenced sections one by one. Skimming past the clinical entries – like a chart on the development of feminine sex-roles in males – I stopped at a paragraph on adolescence.

As I read the text closely, one point jumped off the page. According to *Human Sexuality*, boys *commonly* engaged in homosexual play as a *normal* part of adolescence – a behavior that decreased when the boys approached "full adolescent responsiveness."

They were Jupiter-words, but their meaning was clear to me.

I just had to wait it out.

???

Even with the assurances from *Human Sexuality*, my belly continued to jitter with anxiety. Whenever it did, I headed to the kitchen and stacked a plate with leftover ham, or Pepperidge Farm cake, or whatever snack we had on hand. Late night became my favorite time for these impromptu smorgasbords, to accompany the best TV shows. *The Twilight Zone* was on every night at 11. On the weekends, *The Avengers* and *Sherlock Holmes Mysteries* kept me company into the wee hours.

Anne's friend, Julie, visited for a Friday overnight. I heard them talking in my sister's room as I walked along the upstairs hall. Julie spoke.

"Her son is in eighth grade and weighs 180 pounds. Can you *imagine* a kid that big?"

I pressed my back against the wall near the door and froze. *I* weighed 180.

"Wow," Anne said. "Poor kid."

They moved on to other subjects. I retreated to my bedroom and looked in the mirror on the back of my closet door.

I was huge, almost as big around as Molly or Mom or Dad.

Dieting would fix my problem, any detective could figure that out. Mentally bidding farewell to the Big Fritz, I began the next morning by mixing a protein drink that my mom always drank for breakfast. Powdery flecks clung to the rim of the glass. They tasted chalky on my first sip.

Can you imagine a kid that big? echoed in my head.

Summoning the bloated image of my body in the mirror, I tilted my head and drained the glass. The mixture had thickened near the bottom. I managed to gag it down.

At lunch, I ate a PB&J sandwich accompanied by an apple. No dessert.

After school, I began an exercise regimen in my bedroom, playing my disco forty-fives as incentive. I listed my aerobic activities in my journal. It felt clinical and encouraging.

Thursday, December 13, 1979

Exercises:

> √ *sit ups - 20*
> √ *run stairs (5 up, 5 down)*
> √ *leg lifts - 5*
> √ *jumping jacks - 50*
> √ *Wonder Womans - 25*
> √ *toe touchers - 25*

Friday morning, a week later, I stepped off the bathroom scales, disappointed. I actually felt a little more energetic, but I wasn't noticing any change in my weight. Downstairs, I blended my protein quickly. I couldn't miss the bus; Paul had gone to the store early.

I looked at the cupboard of mom's health supplements. *Should I take some of them as well?* I reviewed the bottles and settled on a multi-vitamin the size of a horse pill. I popped two and chased them with the chalky mixture.

The mass churned in my gut for a few minutes, adjusting to its surroundings as I hurried to gather my books. I burped, tasting a grainy pulp in my mouth. Something wasn't sitting right.

Getting my coat out of the library closet, a wave of nausea flushed through me. I ran to the front door and yanked it open – just in time to spew the contents of my stomach under the front bushes.

I hurried to the kitchen sink to rinse my mouth, then raced for the end of the driveway in time to catch the bus.

I'd never thrown up a Big Fritz.

???

Despite Dad's attempts to keep the honyocks from browsing *Playboy* in the store, they purchased it and stood around the coffee pot, flipping the pages.

To combat the situation, he worked out a better deal. Retiring *Playboy* was the first step. In its place, he bought tightly wrapped cellophane bundles of bargain-priced pornography.

I eliminated the *Playboy* section from behind the counter and reluctantly piled the sealed packets of porn below the magazine rack. Paper inserts on both sides screamed at me – *Adult Magazines, Do Not Open* – blocking any view of the contents.

For a detective of my caliber, the temptation to know what lay beyond the generic label flirted with me throughout each Saturday night shift. The less busy I was, the more I returned to the rack. The lure gnawed at my mind. *Would it be like the Pamela Sue Martin Playboy? Would I have a more normal reaction to it, now that I had the bathtub as guidance?*

I needed to know.

I gathered one of the plastic packages and took it to the back room, listening for the electronic beep to signal a customer's entrance. Rotating the cellophane carefully, I studied the contents. There were at least five magazines inside. Maybe more.

My nail found the edge of the wrap and worked at it. The bundle resisted, but once I got a full finger underneath, the plastic peeled back.

I opened the top with precision, knowing that I'd have to reseal it in exactly the order it came apart. Reaching in, I eased one of the magazines free, working it slowly back and forth to release it from its cocoon of plastic and paper.

Although it had no cover, I quickly identified it as *Playboy*. The features and pictures were similar to the Pamela Sue Martin edition – as was my reaction. Next I pulled out *Hustler*, also coverless. I flipped through the pages of breasts and buttocks, disappointed.

My third pull from the pack brought all distractions to a grinding halt.

A naked man stared back at me. The words *In this issue of Blueboy* floated in a bubble next to his hairy chest.

I turned the pages slowly, my eyes drinking in the images. Men were kissing – and doing other things. *I don't believe this! There's a magazine that shows naked men together.* I finally understood why my friends drooled over Melody's breasts.

Fortunately, no beep from the door chime interrupted me. Rushing to the front door, I spun the lock and posted the "Back in 5 minutes" sign we used for emergencies.

Blueboy and I spent a while in the bathroom.

RUNAWAY PLAN: Cincinnati/Weeks Five— Six (1984)

The first month dragged. Nothing felt in balance. My classes distracted me from my memories of Roy – from my loneliness – but back at the apartment, while Molly worked evenings, only my thoughts, my snacks, and my nighttime habit kept me company.

A fresh Catholic-related guilt wove its way into my days. I'd never embraced a Mass routine in Cincinnati. I wondered what Father O'Malley, my high school English-and-Religion mentor, would think of my elapsed devotion. I probably wouldn't earn a "Gasp! Beautiful!" comment in my religion notebook anymore.

Forcing unpleasant thoughts aside, I focused on daily trips to the apartment's mailbox. Letters arrived often. I couldn't get enough.

I carried the envelopes to the rooftop before I opened them. Comfortable with my beach towel, walkman, and bag of snacks, I read each letter over and over. My best friend, Bob. Father O. My ex-girlfriend, Beth. Everybody talked about Roy's death.

I wrote back to them all – long, philosophical letters about valuing time and cherishing friendship. Without alcohol as inspiration, I became Drinking Dar, pouring onto paper some of the confusion I felt.

I found myself fighting harder to edit out my inner turmoil. Longing for Bob. Attraction to my new neighbor, Danny. The one topic I wouldn't share lurked between the lines.

I reread every paragraph before mailing, ensuring I hadn't slipped somehow.

.

Chapter Eight: Crime Scene 1 (1980)

January 27, 1980
Dear God,
Please help me to be a normal man. It's 3:12AM and I masturbated again. Dear God in Heaven, help me. Give me strength and courage, to be a man, thin, handsome and sexually appealing. Help me to control my urges and have sex with my wife some day.

I took the entrance exam at McQuaid. I think I did OK.

I'm growing up. Lately I've been feeling out of place, weird, and that I don't really know my family. I enjoy going to school and being with my friends.

I love You, God. And I thank You for my wonderful family and my wonderful life.

Thank You, my Father.

THE SOLACE I'D taken from *Human Sexuality* wore thin. I'd been waiting for over two months and my bathtub time was still consumed with thoughts of boys. Movie stars or comic book heroes added steam to my fantasies.

In February, my bathtub habit migrated to my bedroom. Discovering the plush warmth of my blankets and pillows, I imagined being alone with another boy. Sometimes we'd hug, his strong arms pulling me close against a sturdy chest. More often we'd wrestle beneath the covers.

It always ended the same: the explosion of release, the queasy knot in my stomach.

To gather more evidence, I went back to my research. This time I sneaked the "H" encyclopedia from my parents' library and brought it to my room. Behind closed doors, I opened to the topic that troubled me.

Two pages of text listed tons of facts. I read through each paragraph meticulously. The first point to catch my attention said that thirty-seven percent of guys had orgasms with other guys at some point in their life.

Thirty-seven percent? Maybe the feelings *would* pass, like *Human Sexuality* had promised.

The next section told me that in studies of primitive societies, more than sixty percent considered homosexual practice as normal.

Normal? The word leapt off the page at me.

I read on. A heading further down on the page promised to explain the causal factors for homosexuality. *Please help me, Jesus.* I forged ahead.

I quickly learned that scientists couldn't agree whether genes, circumstances during childhood development, encouragement from society, or parental relationships resulted in homosexuality.

The tug-of-war competition in my intestines relaxed slightly. I didn't know about my genes, but I hadn't met any homosexuals in society or had peer-pressure for sex. My family, other than my dad's intermittent anger, was wonderful. *Maybe* I would be okay.

I read the final paragraph. It suggested that the causes might forever remain a topic for debate. They listed other articles as reference, including prison inmate behavior, Israelite elimination, and prostitution.

Elimination? Prison? Prostitution? None of that sounded good. I was glad for the reassurance that these feelings were a normal part of my adolescence – that they would pass.

I'd read enough to know I didn't want to be a homosexual.

???

February 2, 1980

I insulated the roof of HQ today with rug scraps. Hopefully it will keep it warmer in there. I froze listening to Mystery Theater last night.

Yesterday I saw a guy running across the back field and down the farm roads. He jumped in a truck marked "Poultry" and went south on our road. I couldn't get the license plate.

I finally told everybody in my family about Headquarters. I couldn't mask the amount of time I spent in the barn. Besides, I was proud.

Mom and Dad were too large to make the climb, but I brought my siblings up, one at a time. Anne and Kathy admired the desk and work area I'd set up. Mike complimented my improvements, especially the siren, when he visited from Virginia. Molly shared emergency chocolate bars with me when she flew back from Cincinnati.

Even Paul struggled carefully over the grain bin wall one time to check out my agency and listen to *Mystery Theater*. We didn't tell Mom.

I enhanced HQ as I had new ideas. I wanted some kind of first alert mechanism to tell me if intruders were on the property – like the guy who had run across the field and jumped into the poultry truck.

I climbed down through Tunnel Two and looked over the area. Searching through the piles I found a switch box, which I hooked against the wall of the barn. When the massive wooden door slid open along its track, it flicked the switch on. The reverse was true as well.

Linking the device to a flashing black light I'd installed just above my desk in Headquarters, I was ready for testing. I climbed down and slid the heavy door back. The black light flashed its urgent alarm through the open vent hole.

Cool, I thought, liking the Jupiter Jones feel of it.

???

Adam arrived for a Friday overnight to check out my modifications of Headquarters. With eighth grade graduation approaching, our opportunities to get together dwindled. I was probably headed to McQuaid Jesuit in the fall. He would go to the public high school in Arcadia. No more Merk to drive both of us to Big Brick on the Friday-afternoon Saint Mike's bus.

After dinner, we headed to HQ. A winter wind rattled the metal roof just above the ceiling of Headquarters. My space heater strained to warm the tiny area.

I proudly displayed my pornography collection. A pile of magazines had accumulated since my discovery of *Blueboy* in November – the naked girls outnumbering the boys by four to one, keeping pace with the ratio contained in the plastic packages I'd appropriated from Gerard's Grocery. The girl ones, I showed to Adam. The boy ones were well-hidden in the corner.

His eyes widened with appreciation. "Holy cow!" he said. "This is some collection!" I pulled my chair close to him, watching over his shoulder as he flipped through the pages. Even in the chilly air, I was aware of the heat coming through his flannel shirt.

After he'd examined every issue of *Playboy* and *Hustler*, we trudged through the snow drifts that blocked Big Brick's rear sidewalk. Inside, we stripped off our snow gear and went to my room.

"Whattya wanna do now?" he said, as we laid out a sleeping bag on my bedroom floor.

From nowhere, memories of my parent's party came into my head. An idea quickly took shape. "Hey, you wanna have some vodka?" I asked my best friend. "It's kinda fun. I had some last summer. It makes you feel kinda silly."

Anne popped her head into my open bedroom door, causing Adam and me to jump. "And JUST WHERE are you gonna get vodka?" she demanded.

Anne had the bedroom across from mine all to herself – now that Kathy lived in Rochester. Five years older, Anne had just reached the legal drinking age. She'd enjoyed the newfound freedom, sometimes keeping a bottle of alcohol in her bedroom. I knew she had a pint of Smirnoff in her top drawer tucked underneath the white tube socks. My parents didn't know.

"Ummm, your dresser?" I responded, grinning sheepishly.

"Oh re-al-ly," she said, dragging it out. Then she smiled. "Okay, you guys can have some, but I'll do the pouring. Go downstairs and find something to mix it with. And don't tell anybody what you're doing."

I raced to the kitchen. Mom and Dad sat in the family room watching an episode of M*A*S*H. I grabbed a Sunkist orange soda from the refrigerator.

"What are you doing, Honey?" Mom smiled at me over the kitchen counter.

"Just grabbing some pop."

"There's some ice cream left in the freezer, if you and Adam would like some."

"That's okay, we're good for right now, thanks," I cut her off and rushed back up the stairs.

Anne had two plastic glasses on top of her dresser. She poured a quarter inch of alcohol into each, then topped it off with Sunkist. "You're supposed to use orange juice to make a real screwdriver, but this'll be okay.

"Now I want you guys to be careful," she said, holding out the glasses in front of her. "Don't go doing something stupid and end up hurting yourself."

"We'll be fine," I said in my best Jupiter I've-got-a-handle-on-the-situation tone. Adam and I took our glasses and returned to my room.

The vodka made the pop bitter. I gulped mine. Adam worked more slowly at his. In a short while the giddy feeling swirled through my head.

The sleepover took on a silly, grown-up mood that we'd not had previously, when we'd simply played Yahtzee and eaten frozen pizza in the family room. This night, we stayed behind my closed door, cloistered in the conspiracy of imbibing.

"Do you think we'll even remember this?" I asked, drawing on my experiences with Drinking Dar.

"Who knows?" Adam speculated, standing up from the bean bag chair he'd settled into. "Whoaaa," he swayed, "the room is spinning. This is cool!" He rotated on one foot, then fell onto the bed, giggling.

I sat beside him, reaching for the top of his head to give him a noogie. He laughed and skirted my closed fist, twisting to tickle me. We wrestled on the bed for a few minutes until we were out of breath, sweaty on the cold winter evening.

I looked at him, chest heaving in and out, as our bodies mashed together. My excitement grew. I pulled away, embarrassed that he'd notice.

I changed the subject. "Hey, you want some ice cream?"

"Sure."

I sat for a couple of moments on the floor next to the bed, allowing my lungs to inflate – and the rest of me to deflate. Standing, I crept down to the kitchen and opened the freezer. My parents had already gone to bed. I scooped two bowls of ice cream and headed back upstairs.

I found Adam in Anne's room with both of our glasses.

"Okay, just a little more, but this is it. You're cut off," Anne said in her tough-guy tone that told me she meant it. I let the adult feel of the words flush over me.

Cut off.

How cool.

She poured a tiny splash of vodka into each glass and topped it with a hearty amount of Sunkist.

"Thanks," Adam said. He winked at her as though he were ordering drinks in a downtown bar. We grabbed our glasses and headed back to my room.

"We could put our ice cream in our drinks," I said as we started our second screwdriver of the evening. "Sorta like a float."

"Okay," Adam said, as we experimented, forming a thick, creamy mixture that we had to eat with spoons. Soon both glasses stood empty. "What're we gonna do now?" Adam glanced around the room.

I looked at the clock radio. Eleven-thirty. "Let's watch *The Avengers*," I said, suggesting a reason to stay on the bed together. I clicked on the small black and white TV that sat on my dresser.

We settled into my twin mattress to watch the hour-long show. Our heads were close to the tube; our bodies smashed against each other. I was glad to be lying face down. The combination of alcohol and Adam's proximity caused powerful stirrings below my belt.

Anne stopped in once before she went to bed, 'just to make sure we didn't fall out a window or suffocate in our own vomit.'

When the end credits flashed across the screen, I was still enjoying the warmth of Adam next to me. The rest of the household had settled into sleep. I clicked off the set and we prepared for bed.

"I'll sleep on the floor," Adam said, stripping to his underwear and unzipping his sleeping bag.

"Okay," I agreed, pulling off my jeans and shirt. I'd lost my tipsy edge, but my desire remained powerful.

"Let's play Truth or Dare," I suggested.

"Okay," he agreed.

I clicked off my reading lamp. The image of the bulb swirled behind my eyelids for several moments.

I started. "Truth or dare?"

"Truth."

I thought for a minute or so, the residual lightness in my head and darkness of the room making me bolder than normal.

"Do you ever touch your penis?"

He considered my question.

"Yeah, every time I go to the bathroom."

It wasn't the answer I wanted, but it satisfied the rules of the game.

My turn.

"Dare," I said before he had time to ask which I'd prefer.

Adam was quiet for a long time.

"No matter what you ask, I have to do it," I encouraged.

Darkness couldn't mask the desire that engulfed us.

"Suck my dick," he said abruptly.

An electric shock shot through my tensed body. "What?"

"You heard me."

I considered his proposal, my heart rocketing wildly in my chest. "If I do that, you'd probably tell somebody."

"No, I wouldn't."

"You promise you won't tell anybody?" My thoughts raced to keep ahead of the anxious excitement that rushed into my groin. I'd dreamed about it, longed for it but, presented with the opportunity, I was afraid.

My stomach danced in circles.

"I'm drunk, I probably won't even remember it happened," he offered.

The words from the encyclopedia flashed in my head.

Thirty-seven percent of guys had orgasms with other guys at some point in their life.

I got out of my bed and lay with him on the floor of my room for a long while.

I woke to see crisp frost patterns on the window pane, sparkling in the eastern sunlight.

I looked at Adam, his naked body covered with a thick sleeping bag. His flannel shirt, jeans, and underwear lay in a heap nearby. Jaws of guilt clenched at my abdomen, bringing me physical pain. I plodded to the bathroom and stared into the mirror. My hair clumped in a wild, tangled mass. Lower, my belly jutted over the edge of my underwear, obscuring the waistband.

Nothing looked different.

Back in my bedroom, I pulled on my jeans and a sweatshirt. Adam stirred, but he didn't waken. I tiptoed out of the room holding my breath. My head felt cloudy, like I'd been prepping for a final exam. *Is this a hangover?* I wondered.

I thought about last night. How we didn't need any more dares to try lots of things in the dark. How the metallic feel of his braces had surprised me *down there*.

Mom was already feeding the Opes when I reached the kitchen. "Hi, Honey," she said, humming as she mixed the Quaker oatmeal. "Would you like some Mother's Oats?" she asked.

I wonder why she always calls them that? my mind drifted.

"No thanks," I said, popping some bread into the toaster. "My stomach's upset."

"I'm sorry, Honey," she turned her attention to me. "Why don't you try an apple? Mum always said they settle an upset tummy."

"I think I'll just have some toast."

I wondered what she'd say if she knew what Adam and I had done. *And that I enjoyed it.*

Mom doled out the oatmeal and carried the tray toward the Opes' kitchen. I stacked eight buttered pieces of toast onto a plate and, grabbing the peanut butter jar and a knife, headed into the family room to watch cartoons. *The Bugs Bunny/Roadrunner Hour* was on. I settled deep into the couch.

Adam came down an hour later.

"Hi," he said.

"Hi," I replied.

I studied the rust-colored carpet while he walked through to the kitchen. He grabbed a box of cereal and pulled a bowl out of the cupboard.

"You wanna go snowmobiling?" he ventured. Adam wasn't scheduled to go home until one o'clock, after Paul finished playing a wedding. If the bride and groom invited my brother to eat with them, it might be even later. I mentally calculated the hours until Adam would be gone.

"No, my stomach's upset."

I didn't move from the couch and was grateful that he sat out of sight at the kitchen table. "You go ahead if you want," I said.

"You sure?"

"Yeah."

My mom entered the kitchen from the hallway door. She carried the conversation with Adam through the rest of his cereal.

129

He set his empty bowl into the sink and went to don his blue vinyl snowsuit. Before going out, he stopped by the family room one more time.

"You *sure* you don't want to go snowmobiling?" He sounded genuinely surprised that I refused.

I looked into his eyes, searching for any sign that an alcohol-induced blackout had robbed him of what we'd shared.

His face was unreadable.

"Yeah, my stomach really hurts."

It did.

"Arrright," he shrugged and headed out to the barn.

Paul came back from the wedding on time and took Adam home. I didn't ride along, my gut still ached.

Sunday, March 16, 1980
Dear Diary,
I haven't seen you for awhile.
Ever since that gay experience with Adam, I kind of hate him.
I was accepted to McQuaid. I don't know if I'll go or not.

???

Jesus of Nazareth, a four-night miniseries, played on TV the whole week before Easter. I didn't miss a minute.

I knew the story from church. We Catholics heard the Passion of Christ read aloud every year. To *see it* was different. More personal.

When Jesus hung on the cross – which I knew was for sinners like me – my heart swelled up with regret and love for Him. I quietly wiped tears from the corners of my eyes, hoping Mom or Paul didn't notice.

The following night, I climbed into HQ and looked at my collection of magazines. Tonight, the pile was a smutty stack of filth – Jesus had died a miserable death and I looked at pictures of naked men.

Guilt about what I'd done with Adam rollercoasted through my abdomen.

From my pocket, I pulled the black plastic garbage bag I'd brought from the kitchen. I shook it until it billowed wide, then began dumping the magazines inside.

In fifteen minutes it was done. I struggled to seal the bulging bag. Dragging it to the ladder, I hoisted it to the roof of HQ and hefted it onto the stage. It landed with an enormous *whumphh*; a cloud of dust rose. Wings flapped madly overhead as the pigeons relocated to the south end of the barn.

Tomorrow was garbage day. I made sure to seal the sack tightly before I tossed it into the back of our dumpster. I threw a few cardboard boxes on top of it, to ensure its anonymity.

The next morning, I watched out my bedroom window as the garbage truck hoisted the dumpster into the air. The truck's hydraulics screamed in protest. Our week's worth of trash – and my entire porn collection – disappeared into the bowels of the vehicle.

I silently vowed to stop my nightly ritual.

???

Our cream-colored '72 Ford station wagon was one of my father's favorite cars. Like the other used vehicles he'd purchased, it had some spots of decay, some tricks to fire the ignition. Both rear wheel wells had rusted through, allowing tire spray to soak the back area. At only 120,000 miles, the engine ran smoothly, but when Dad made a grocery run to the city on a damp day, the supplies returned covered with muck. He grudgingly bought a used Mercury wagon and parked the Ford behind the barn.

An afternoon near my fourteenth birthday, Dad entered the kitchen, where I munched Oreos. He pulled a small box from his pocket and slapped it onto the table in front of me.

"Hey Caboose," he said, "this is for you."

I opened it quickly, the cookies somersaulting in my stomach.

The keys to the Ford lay inside.

I blinked.

"For me?!"

"Yup. I can't use it on the road anymore, but I thought you'd get a kick out of driving it around the farm roads behind the barn."

"Wow! *Thanks!*"

It was all I could muster through my surprise.

"Just remember, a car's not a toy. You're pushing a ton of American rolling iron every time you step on the pedal."

"I'll be careful!"

I would have promised anything. Despite all his detective success, Jupiter didn't own a car.

"Let's take it for a spin," he said. We headed out the back door. "You can drive," he directed, when I headed for the passenger seat. "Now you're familiar with the accelerator, brake, gear shift?"

I was.

"Ease us out nice and slow, 'til you get the hang of it. Take a swing around the circle and then we'll try out behind the barn."

The pedals responded quicker than I'd expected, but under his guidance, I tested pushing the gas, hitting the brakes. The next half hour I worked to find the feel of it, tooling around the farm roads, dredging up small clouds of dust as we drove.

It was the coolest thing my dad had ever done for me. I sifted through the experience with pleasant disbelief.

???

Friday April 11, 1980

Today ends a two-week vacation from school. I had a good Easter. I got my car from Dad last week. I'm only 13, but it's fun. I moved the CB radio from HQ to the car and mounted speakers on the roof, just like a real police car. Now when I talk through the "PA" setting on the CB, it comes out through the speakers!

I still haven't talked much with Adam. Things feel funny with him now.

Before Easter, we went to confession with Father Deckman. I confessed disrespect of my body. But on Thursday before Easter, I sinned again with masturbation. I have started again. I pray to God that I can stop, but when I'm doing it, I try to avoid God so I won't stop. It's kind of like saying you'll diet after a big meal.

My Jesus of Nazareth vow had succumbed to the lure of my nighttime habit. In the steamy minutes before sleep, I thought about different guys. Sometimes Adam. Sometimes Superman. Sometimes Frank or Joe Hardy.

The highs that accompanied my moaning pleasure were quickly followed by revulsion, the pit of my stomach clenching tight.

I had to know what Jesus thought about my secret.

We'd received a Catholic Study Bible at Saint Mike's in fifth-grade religion class. I still had it, somewhere under my bed. Digging through the pile of mystery books and M&M wrappers, I located the thick volume.

I turned to the index. The "S" section seemed an appropriate place to start. *Seventy, Severe, Shade* – no *Sex*.

Next I tried the "H" section.

No *Homosexuality*.

With methodical resolve, I started at the beginning, scanning page by page. I turned through Genesis quickly. We'd been through that in Sister Helen's Religion class – I didn't remember any homos in there.

Exodus was all about Moses, I knew that story by heart.

In Leviticus, the tales got juicier. Laws about holiness. I slowed my pace.

The title of Chapter 18 halted my investigation: *Forbidden Sexual Practices*. My eyes jumped through the text.

Do not have intercourse with a woman during her monthly period, because she is ritually unclean.

"Yuck," I said to no one.

Do not have intercourse with another man's wife; that would make you ritually unclean.

I skipped down.

No man is to have sexual relations with another man; God hates that.

My insides tightened, as though I'd just heard my father yell my name from the bottom of the stairs. I sat back, digesting the words.

God hates that.

I glanced to the next page. *Penalties for Disobedience.* My hand shook as I traced the sentences. I stopped in the middle of the next paragraph.

If a man lies with a man as with a woman, both of them shall be put to death for their abominable deed; they have forfeited their lives.

I shut my eyes and the book as well.

Man lies with a man. I could still see the words behind my lids. A*bominable.* It was worse than what Father Fredricks had said about desecrating our bodies. I was an abomination in the eyes of Jesus? I knew what it meant – *man lies with a man* – I'd had the night with Adam.

Tasting something like battery acid in my mouth, I hurried downstairs to make a sundae.

That night, I tried to rationalize the impact of what I'd read in the Bible versus my earlier research.

Human Sexuality had said that my feelings were normal, that I'd grow beyond them.

The encyclopedia seemed confusing, with its doubletalk about normalcy and prison behavior in the same section.

And now Jesus thought the whole thing was an *abomination*.

I finally drifted into an uneasy sleep, assuring myself that my attraction to Adam, to other boys, to Superman, would soon fade. That my struggling would stop when I reached *full adolescent responsiveness*.

Until then, I would offer it up.

Saturday, April 12, 1980

I worked at Gerard's Grocery today from 1 – 9. I closed the store for 5 min. and jerked off in the bathroom. I can't believe I am so susceptible to temptation. If I were to simply pray when I get these urges, I would be able to resist them.

Dear Jesus, give me strength to make it through this period of my life, though I be so unworthy. Please forgive my sins, and help me to grow in Your Spirit for ever and ever, amen.

Thank you, Lord.

???

My fourteenth birthday arrived. I had to wait until almost nine o'clock to open my gifts; Drinking Dar insisted on making a special salad for dinner and the project dragged on for more than two hours.

My favorite present came from Anne: A hard cover copy of *The Dead Zone*, the newest book from Stephen King.

I'd discovered his horror books earlier that year when a kid on the bus loaned me *Salem's Lot*. Within a couple of months, I'd also read *The Shining* and *The Stand*. They weren't mystery stories, but I loved the characters and the scary things that happened to them. *The Twilight Zone* come to life.

"Who's Stephen King?" my father asked, turning the book over and over.

"A writer I like," I said, cringing as salad oil from his fingers left grease marks on the book jacket.

"It'll wipe off," Anne whispered in my ear.

???

Thursday, June 19, 1980

Well, it's come and gone. I'm no longer a grade schooler.

We had our Saint Michael's graduation tonight. After graduation Mass, Fr. Deckman took me aside and said, "You're not ready for this yet, and I don't know why I'm saying this to you, but I think you should consider entering a seminary."

Now I don't know where to turn.

God, give me guidance. Lead me through life.

???

Drinking Dar was a long-winded philosopher, proper and proud, anxious to carry on the intimate conversations he avoided the rest of the time. When live company eluded him, he turned to writing, penning long, eloquent letters to different people. Tonight, he sat at the kitchen table, writing a letter on a yellow legal pad. *Probably to one of his aunts in California*, I thought.

I headed up to my room above the kitchen. Paul was at the store late, so I skipped *Mystery Theater*, preferring to read *The Dead Zone*.

I heard Dad below, pulling the scotch from the liquor cabinet. The bottle clinked against his glass. Next, the big freezer door sucked open, the one near the hall.

Ice, I thought.

A loud crash shook the wall behind my headboard.

Then silence.

Throwing back my comforter, I raced down the stairs. Anne was close behind.

My father crouched in the kitchen doorway, his head and hands both leaning heavily on the jamb just a couple of feet above the floor. He let out a heavy sigh and tried to pull himself up, unsuccessfully.

"What happened?" I shouted, out of breath.

"I lost my balance." He tried to stand, but his considerable bulk and awkward position in the doorway made the attempt unsuccessful. I went around through the family room and propped my hand under his armpit. Anne supported the other side, like we did with the Old People. We raised him.

"No problem, nothing broken," he said, tottering back to the kitchen table. "I'll probably head up to bed." Anne and I looked at each other, then scurried upstairs to talk.

"Do you think he's okay?" I asked.

"Yeah." She didn't sound as certain as usual. "I don't think he hurt himself."

"Should we go tell Mom?"

"Nahh, she's gotta get up and feed the Opes. Besides, he should be okay now that he's going to bed."

???

In August, after the flurry of Mormon season had passed, I decided to throw a graduation party for the kids from my Saint Michael's class. It would be good to see them one last time before high school began. Especially Adam – I hadn't resolved what had happened between us. Maybe a party atmosphere would set everything straight.

The Friday of the party, kids arrived by the carload. Adam, Gaila, Melody, and other Saint Mike's friends. I invited Caroline from across the street to join us. As a group, we swam in the pool, then played hide and seek in the corn field.

As the sky turned dusky, people gathered at the fire pit in Big Brick's backyard. I looked around for Adam. He wasn't in sight.

"Where's Adam?" I asked a friend.

He laughed. "Somebody brought a pint bottle of Southern Comfort. I think he and some of the guys went behind the barn to polish it off." Caroline, who sat close enough to hear, looked at me and frowned.

"It's okay," I said to my younger friend at the same time my mind raced with the information. *Adam is drinking. Adam could get drunk. If Adam gets drunk, he might tell what we did.* My gut seized.

The Saint Mike's kid must have seen a change in my face. "Relax, Greg, it's not like they're gonna get smashed or get you into trouble with your folks or something," he said.

I tried to think quickly without showing *too much* concern – someone might figure out that I was hiding something. *Should I go look for them? People might think that's weird.* A group activity would divert attention. "Okay, everybody!" I said at the top of my lungs. "Time to tell ghost stories!"

For the next twenty minutes, I tried to keep the contents of my stomach settled as one kid after another made up spooky tales. Some were funny, some were scary, but I had trouble enjoying any of them. *The longer they're gone, the more they'll drink.*

Adam and three other classmates, two boys and one girl, finally came around the side of the barn and joined us at the fire pit. They plopped down hard in the grass and giggled. I searched my friend's face for any hint of betrayal, but through the firelight's flickering glow, I could only see his tipsy smirk.

A short while later, parents began showing up in station wagons. We all stood up from the grass and said our goodbyes.

I approached Adam. The tipsy edge seemed gone from his smile. Now he just looked tired. "See ya, Greg," he said.

I stared at him. *Had he told?* I had no way to know – and no way to ask. "See ya," I said.

I watched them all, including Adam, pile into several cars, wave goodbye, and pull down Big Brick's winding drive. An emotional soup still simmered in my stomach, but it was soothed with an unhappy relief that I'd never have to see Adam again.

RUNAWAY PLAN: Cincinnati/Week Seven (1984)

In late September, my parents and Paul drove from Rochester to Cincinnati to visit Molly and me. In the hours before they arrived, we raced from room to room, picking up clothes, fast food wrappers, and empty soda cans. By Friday evening, the place sparkled. We even removed the soaking-in-turpentine brushes from the kitchen cupboard.

"Oh—it's—lovely—Honey," Mom said, catching her breath as she looked around the apartment. She'd stopped twice on the way up the stairs. Paul had made it up without breathing hard – he was one of the thinner Gerards – although his limp was pronounced as he walked around the apartment.

He and I had exchanged letters since our awkward hug goodbye, but, like everything else from back home, he felt somehow distant to me. We'd never again talk on Radio Shack phones between our bedrooms at Big Brick. We'd never again visit Perkins on the way to Saint Mike's. My chest felt an embarrassed ache I couldn't pinpoint to any one spot.

"You get used to the climb," I said, shifting away from the thoughts I couldn't express.

We spent Saturday showing them around town, starting with a featured tour of Xavier.

"Oh, I always wanted to go to college on a beautiful campus," Mom said, looking at the sprawling green lawn which ended at the tall stone chapel. "Is that where we'll go to church?"

"Sure, there's a ten o'clock service on Sundays," I said quickly, recalling the poster I'd seen. They'd be shocked to know I hadn't been to Mass in two months. Molly didn't attend either. I prayed they wouldn't ask the priest's name.

"So where's the campus Perkins?" Paul joked. I rolled my eyes, although I was grateful for the diversion.

Next I toured them through downtown and parked at the river's edge. "I come here sometimes," I said, waving my arm at the brown water below us. "It helps me think."

Mom looked over the scene. "Oh Honey, it's beautiful. Now, you're careful, aren't you? There's no railing down there, it looks like you could drive right off into the water!"

I rolled my eyes again. "Yessss, Mother, I'm careful," I dragged out my phrasing, turning the car back on.

"It all looks good, Caboose," Dad said as I pulled Bufford away from the curb.

Back at the apartment, Mom read the sign on the wall aloud. "Park at your own risk." A frown tightened across her face. I waited for her to voice another concern, but my father spoke first.

"Yeah," Dad joked. "Park at your own risk – and run like hell for the door."

"Darwin," Mom scolded as we all laughed.

They left early Monday so they'd make it back to Rochester in the daylight. Watching Paul wave from the back seat of my dad's mammoth Chrysler, my insides constricted. Something about all three of them leaving me in Cincinnati felt exponentially lonelier than when I'd left them at Big Brick just six weeks before.

Chapter Nine: Crime Scene 2 (1980 continued)

THE FIRST DAY of high school rapidly approached. No more Arcadia. No more Big Fritz. I was going to the city.

Anne had arranged to drive me to school every day on her way to the local community college; since we lived so far from the city, McQuaid did not provide a bus for me.

We prepared. Anne organized her college book bag and waxed her '76 Maverick, the latest addition to our family's used car collection. I tried on the new suit Mom had bought for me. Country Clothiers had gone out of business, so we'd picked out my school clothes at J.C. Penny's. I didn't miss hearing comments on my increased size from the Country Clothiers clerk.

The suit was more formal than what I'd worn to Saint Michael's, but I knew high school would bring many differences. I stretched out the stiff material and tried to be comfortable, offering up the itchy feeling I felt underneath the starched garment.

On the Wednesday morning after Labor Day, Anne called up the stairs. "Greg, we gotta go!"

"I'm almost ready," I yelled, frantically pulling the newly tailored pants over my ample behind. I knotted the tie, then yanked it apart in disgust when it ended up hanging below my crotch.

I gave up and raced out of the house. *I'll finish it in the car.*

"Now, listen," she said as we wound down Big Brick's curving drive. "I can't be late for my classes, so we need to leave by eight at the *latest.*" I looked at my watch. The display read 8:04. My stomach crunched.

"Okay. What about me? Am I gonna be late?" The paperwork in my book bag said I had to report to homeroom by eight forty.

"Don't worry about it. I'll get you there on time. I promise." She pulled out of the driveway and the car pitched forward. I relaxed and worked on my tie. When Anne promised something, she meant it.

141

It was a new thing for me to spend time alone with Anne. I sensed that she missed Mike, but I knew her toughness would never let her admit it. She cruised through every yellow light and passed every pokey car. We pulled into the circle behind my new high school thirty-two minutes later.

"I'll see you at Kathy's around four," she said and sped away. We'd arranged our pickup plan in advance: I would walk to Kathy's apartment – Twelve Corners was only two miles away. Anne would meet me there after her last class.

I turned and quickly surveyed the campus where I'd spend the next four years. McQuaid was brick, but not the darkened red of Big Brick. Auburn squares formed the long, low walls, interrupted at regular intervals by metal windows. It was four times as large as Saint Michael's. Instead of nuns, Jesuit priests manned the classrooms.

I'd been to my new school for an orientation day a couple of weeks before and I'd paid careful attention to room numbers and hallway layout. As any good detective would. Passing an outdoor statue of the Virgin Mary, I whispered a prayer and rushed in the closest doorway.

I made it to my homeroom on time, following a map I'd received in my orientation packet. Taking one of the few remaining seats, I watched the priest write his name on the board. I tensed, remembering what Father Fredricks had written just a year earlier on Sister Emily's board. At the same time, an unexpected flash of nostalgia for Saint Michael's bit me.

"I'm Father Jameson," the priest said. "Welcome to McQuaid."

While he talked about our schedule, the school's layout, and how Saint Ignatius Loyola had founded the Jesuit order, I glanced at the other kids.

All boys, they each wore suits similar to mine, looking crisp and groomed for the first day. Their smooth, casual expressions suggested they already knew everything Father Jameson told us. The breakfast cereal I'd gulped down earlier tumbled around my stomach, threatening to resurface.

"Since the weather is so warm, you're all excused from wearing your suit coats until October first." Our homeroom teacher's lips expanded into a thin grin. "Enjoy yourselves!"

I read through my course schedule and determined I needed to be in Geometry first. I stopped at my locker and stashed my notebooks and suit coat. The view down the hall looked out of balance. No girls with checkered skirts and high-pitched laughter. Just a sea of boys.

I pushed my way through, wondering if my body, surrounded by so many guys, would betray me. That they'd pass me and somehow suspect what I thought about at night. McQuaid didn't seem like the kind of place where my inner turmoil would be easing up anytime soon.

Father Chereli taught Geometry wearing the same black shirt and stiff white collar as Father Jameson. He was younger, however, and his tiny square mustache reminded me of crooks who sometimes showed up in mystery shows on Saturday-afternoon TV.

He described the advanced course structure – we would work from an outline. Each section was self-paced. He gave us an overview of the course, welcomed us to McQuaid, then sat behind his desk.

Everyone else began reading and scratching figures on paper, as though someone had pulled each of them aside before I'd arrived, explaining the details of what to do.

At Saint Michael's, we'd never learned without a teacher's instruction. In the city, guys apparently worked on their own. *They probably all like girls, too,* I thought, more bitterly than I'd expected.

A deluge of nostalgia flooded my mind. For Sister Helen and her lively guitar picking. For Perkins trips with my brother. For Adam.

I felt my cheeks flush.

A tap on my shoulder brought me back to McQuaid. "Can I borrow your ruler?"

I turned to look at the boy behind me. He wore thick glasses like mine. His long brown hair cascaded over the top of the frames. I remembered he'd been the only student to arrive in the room later than I. "My name's John," he said.

"Hi, I'm Greg."

We talked in low tones the rest of the period, passing my ruler back and forth as we worked through the first chapter.

Between third and fourth period, I rushed back to my locker to drop off the textbooks I'd collected that morning. I set the stack on the floor, freeing my hands to work the padlock. With the door open, I squatted – and heard a loud tearing sound.

Shocked, I straightened up, then felt my rear end. The new suit pants had split up the seam from the crotch to the beltline! My heart pounded frenetically underneath my tie. *What would Jupiter do?* Anne wasn't picking me up until four. *How could I get through the rest of the school day – AND to the apartment – like this?* I had two minutes to get to my next class.

With no time to come up with a better solution, I grabbed my navy suit coat from inside the locker and wrapped it around my waist, tying the sleeves around my front.

John, the boy who borrowed my ruler, was in my next class, Latin. He came in breathing hard, just as the door closed, and took the desk next to me. He glanced at the suit coat sleeves tied around my beltline and raised an eyebrow. "You know, we don't have to wear our suit coats until October."

I leaned toward him. "I split my pants putting my books in my locker," I whispered. We both chuckled until the teacher called us to order.

The walk from McQuaid to Twelve Corners seemed much longer than thirty minutes with a suit coat tied around my waist. When I arrived at the apartment, I searched through Kathy's closet and found a pair of stretchable sweat pants. They were much smaller than anything I normally wore, but I felt more comfortable in them than my damaged suit.

Anne showed up right on time. "So how was your first day?" she asked. I held up my suit pants, looking at her through the tear in the seat. We both started to laugh.

Wednesday, September 24, 1980

Tonight Anne and I were wrestling (just fooling around) and, after I lost the match and my belly was hanging out from underneath my shirt, she blurted out that she felt sorry for me because I was fat.

It really astonished me. I can't believe she's been thinking this. Am I really that fat? Looking in the mirror tonight, I think I look pretty gross. And I've been thinking of making out with Melody or Gaila. What a joke!

???

Missing our a.m. Perkins time, Paul and I sometimes went out on school nights, combining late-night snacks with organ rehearsal.

An ear musician like Dad, Paul had started playing at Saint Patrick's at sixteen. I enjoyed the status this afforded me. I got to climb the stairs up to the choir loft, even if it was closed to other parishioners. I assisted with small church tasks, like setting the numbers on the hymn board or laying out music for the choir.

On a Wednesday night, Paul invited me to join him at Saint Pat's. He wanted to play the new organ Father McFarland had purchased. We would go to Perkins afterwards.

In spite of Anne's recent assessment, I agreed to both invitations.

In the choir loft, I watched Paul's feet pump the long wooden pedals under the bench, playing louder than when parishioners filled the pews. He worked through the older hymns, his favorites like *Panis Angelicus* and *Onward Christian Soldiers*, songs that had fallen out of favor after Vatican II.

I wandered down the stairs and mingled with the shadows between the statues, letting the music wash over me, feeling holy and blessed and privileged to be alive. I felt the same calming warmth I'd experienced in the field behind the barn.

I approached the altar, knelt, and thought about my life. About what Anne had said. About kissing girls. About Adam.

Focusing on the tabernacle, I begged Jesus to help me with my mixed-up feelings. My sin. To help me find my way.

"I don't know what to do, Lord, other than to offer it up. I am so weak. Jesus, I trust in You."

I whispered the last part out loud. In the stillness of Saint Pat's, with my oldest brother's organ music swelling around me, I sensed His quiet reassurance.

Monday, November 3, 1980

Tonight I started exercising again – and I am saying the Rosary again for the conversion of sinners. I don't look gross! This is the way God made me.

???

My friendship with John from McQuaid grew.

His tardiness worried me. His arrival times at Geometry and Latin continued to push the limits. I watched his striped sports coat flapping back and forth as he rushed down the hall to classes.

Being on the other side of a closed classroom door meant a trip to the vice-principal's office for a late slip – which also came with detention. JUG, the Jesuits called it.

"What's 'JUG' stand for? Does it mean 'in the jug', like what crooks call prison?" I whispered to John. He'd arrived out of breath – just as Father Chereli closed the door. John had already attended JUG three times.

He looked at me and spoke with mock intensity. "*Justice Under God.*"

"Ohhh brother!" I moaned. We both cracked up.

146

John and I shared religion class with Father Jameson. Over the last few weeks we'd studied *The Book of Genesis*: Creation, Cain and Abel, Noah. Today we learned about Sodom and Gomorrah.

Father Jameson read out loud. "*The men of Sodom surrounded the house. All the men of the city, both young and old, were there. They called out to Lot and asked, 'Where are the men who come to stay with you tonight? Bring them out to us!' The men of Sodom wanted to have sex with them.*"

Father Jameson glanced over the book's rim at us, raising one eyebrow. He continued. *"Lot went outside and closed the door behind him. He said to them, 'Friends, I beg you, don't do such a wicked thing!'*

The priest looked across the class, at John, at *me*, a sober smirk spreading across his face. His second eyebrow rose. "*That. Was. Their. Sin.*" Each word came out like a complete sentence.

Waves of fear shot through my chest. *Did he suspect something about me?* My mind raced. Assuming my most neutral expression – as Jupiter might, if cornered by crooks – I listed while Father continued on about the fiery destruction of the doomed city. He offered no further commentary, but his eyebrows continued to rise and fall with the action of the story. The words *justice under God* echoed in my head as I worked to quell the shaking in my stomach.

???

In mid-November, an early snow fell, coating the tips of the grass blades across the five acres around Big Brick. I turned on the space heater in Headquarters and looked through the new pile of magazines I'd collected.

It had begun small. Unable to resist the lure, I'd brought home just one pack of the *Adult Magazines – Do Not Open* in my book bag. Then another. Then a third.

In every pack, there were still four magazines filled with pictures of naked women. Those I set aside. The fifth contained pictures of men. *Blueboy, PlayGirl, Mandate.* I examined them carefully in the privacy of the grain bin, then tucked them underneath the hardware shelf. The girlie magazines I left out in open view on my desk.

I thought about Father Jameson's recent speech and my Jesus-of-Nazareth resolve to squelch that part of my life – the magazines, the nightly release – but I forced the topic out of my mind as quickly as it entered.

My gut churned in response.

???

In early December, I manned the store on a Tuesday night. Normally I only worked Saturdays during the school year, but Paul had to play a special Advent service at church. Dad had worked all day, so The Booker asked me to fill in.

To pass the time between customers, I called John. We swapped stories about freshman year. How Father Jameson raised his eyebrows when he read the Bible. How Father Chereli ignored us during Geometry.

The electronic beep sounded as a tall, broad-shouldered man entered. I asked John to hang on and set the receiver on the back counter.

The customer approached the register. "Are you the only one here?"

"Yeah," I said, my Catholic honesty kicking in before my Three Investigators caution.

He stepped back and, with his left hand, yanked down the gray ski mask that was clumped above his matted hair. Only his eyes and mouth remained. From behind a bulky leg, his right hand appeared. It held a shotgun – which he pointed at me.

"Give me all the money, NOW!" he screamed.

Shock iced through me, as though I'd stepped into Gee's walk-in cooler without any clothes on. I jerked open the cash drawer. My shaking hands struggled to grasp the bills from beneath the metal clips.

148

"Hurry up!" he yelled, shifting back and forth from one leg to the other. I turned to face him, a wad of money clutched in my hand.

The gun barrel stared back.

"Put it in a bag!" he commanded. I complied, filling a small brown bag, the same kind we used for the two fried eggs. He snatched the sack from my hand.

"Get down on the floor! NOW!" he barked, matching the tone my dad used when he ranted most loudly. I sat down behind the counter. The man darted toward the door. A beep from the electric eye signaled his departure.

My breath came in rapid gasps as I waited for shots, or screams, or any other sounds from outside. There was nothing.

I sat, not sure what to do, not wanting to move. I glanced toward the phone. The receiver rested on the counter where I'd left it. *John!* I inched up slowly, looking carefully out the edge of the front window. The crook was nowhere in sight.

I grabbed the phone. "John, I just got robbed!"

"Yeah, right," he replied.

"I gotta go, I gotta call the cops!" I hung up without hearing his reply and dialed the number on the bright yellow sticker above the phone.

"Ontario County sheriff," a man's voice spoke.

"I'm at Gerard's Grocery and I just got ROBBED!" I yelled into the handset.

"Are you okay?" the officer asked.

"Yeah, the guy's gone now."

"We'll have a car there in just a couple of minutes. Stay on the phone 'til they get there and tell me what happened."

I went through it with him, my breaths beginning to slow. Before I'd gotten to the end, a siren sounded in the distance. It became two distinct wails as a couple of cars skidded across the icy pavement into the driveway, their red lights flashing an official surrealism through the windows.

Inside my head, I replayed the scene. The mask. The gun. My hands continued to tremble.

From deep within my gut, a sense of Jupiter surfaced. This was a real crime! Not something my Gram had told me. Not something I'd read in *True Detective*. I was now a victim – but also a witness. Grabbing a piece of paper while still talking to the officer, I considered what facts the First Investigator would capture. A physical description of the criminal. The amount of cash stolen. As I wrote, my hands stopped shaking.

I hung up the phone as several policemen entered. They fired questions at me. *What did he look like? Did I see where he went? Did I hear a car start up after he left?* One of them spoke into his police radio as I described the man. "We're looking for a white male. In his thirties. He may be on foot and may have a shotgun. Over."

"We're on it," a voice replied.

Ready Freddy, our customer/cop, appeared from outside. He wore street clothes, so he'd probably come over from his house. I welcomed the familiar face.

Fred surveyed the scene and blinked rapidly at me, at the other cops, at the empty cash drawer. "I'll call your dad," he said.

As he rushed toward the phone, it rang. He picked it up and nodded back at me. As he spoke, a few policemen went back outside to comb the area, while others congregated around me.

Fred hung up the phone and came back to my side. "That was your dad. I guess the friend you were talking to during the robbery called your parents and told them what happened. Your dad'll be right over."

A new wave of anxiety flooded into my gut. *I wonder if Dad's been drinking,* I thought. *If he's drunk, will they give him a ticket for drunk driving?* I picked up the paper where I'd written my detective notes and focused on reading them to the police.

My father appeared ten minutes later. As far as I could tell, he was just "Dad," not Drinking Dar. I was glad to see him.

"So they hauled you out tonight?" he spoke to Fred, joining the circle of men around me.

"I heard it on the scanner, Dar, so I threw on my duds and came right over. This is a *damn* shame!"

I told my story again, stopping frequently to answer all of their questions.

Almost an hour later, after they'd documented everything, the cops left, assuring us they'd do everything they could to solve the crime.

Dad and I climbed into his Mercury station wagon. "Big happenings, huh Caboose?" he asked.

"Yeah."

"That's a *hell* of a way to end a Tuesday night."

"Yeah," I agreed.

As we raced along the pitch-black frozen roads, without prompting, my mind drifted to the rest of Father Jameson's story from the Bible.

Suddenly the Lord rained burning sulphur on the cities of Sodom and Gomorrah and destroyed them and the whole valley.

A knot of fear and shame dug into the pit of my stomach.

Part Three: Deductions

"*When you have excluded the impossible, whatever remains, however improbable, must be the truth.*"

~*Sherlock Holmes,*
The Adventures of Sherlock Holmes

Cast of Characters

Sheena Easton: An attractive Scottish singer; her physical presence *just might* jump-start Greg's heterosexuality

Bob: A tanned sportsman who likes basketball and backrubs

Father O'Malley: An actor from *The Exorcist* with a personalized portrait of Sophia Loren on his classroom wall

Beth: A girl from the all-female Catholic school across town; she teaches Greg more about French kissing than he wants to know

Father Hubert: A high school counselor whose gaze cuts through clouds of cigarette smoke

Roy: Greg's rafting buddy who'd rather be listening to The Police

Father Keneally: A college counselor well-versed in motivational phrases

Jupiter, the Roman God of Lightning: His bolts of punishment strike dead those mortals who are an abomination in his sight

Chapter Ten: Triangulation (1983)

"WHAT'S A SHEENA EASTON?" my brother, Paul, asked, after I set up my new record on display in my bedroom.

I laughed. "A Scottish singer I like."

"Uh *huh*," he said. "And for this she gets a shrine?"

I laughed again. "I think she's pretty."

"Uh *huh*," he repeated, then headed back to his own room.

After my brother left, I sat on the yellow shag carpet in my bedroom and studied my collection. Sheena Easton had debuted on the U.S. pop charts two years earlier. Her first single, *Morning Train*, hit number one.

Something about her voice captured me – sometimes soft, sometimes powerful, always packed with drama. Her next releases, *Modern Girl*, *You Could Have Been With Me*, and *When He Shines* had all become my favorites. I now owned album, cassette, and forty-five versions of all her songs.

Pulling her newest forty-five off my display, I put the record on my bedroom turntable. As it spun, I pulled down her first album and studied the picture on the cover of her perky hair, her penetrating eyes.

Was this what it felt like to be attracted to girls?

She belted out *For Your Eyes Only*, no trace of an accent in her lyrics. I turned the album cover over and drank in her dark, broody features.

She was the prettiest woman I'd ever seen.

I placed the record jacket on the floor in front of me and stared at the picture. *Maybe this is it*, I thought. *Guys liking chicks. I'm sixteen now. Maybe it's time.* I willed my body to stir.

Nothing.

I didn't let this lack of progress below my belt squelch the excitement I felt higher up. She was *so* beautiful. The shift I'd been praying for – my normal attraction to girls, my *full adolescent responsiveness* – seemed to be flirting with me, almost within my grasp after all these years. *Human Sexuality*'s promise coming through.

I played the record over and over, singing along with a renewed hope.

???

I was now a junior at McQuaid. In my two years there, I'd gotten used to being taught by priests instead of nuns. Also, instead of being transported by Paul or Anne, I now drove to school every day in my '77 Plymouth Fury, a car my family had inherited when an elderly relative passed away. My own Ford station wagon had died years earlier, belching engine oil onto the farm roads behind the barn.

Over burgers, John – my freshman-year friend who still ran ten minutes behind the rest of the world – and I had dubbed my new vehicle "Bufford," in honor of its wide chassis and old-man charm.

My sister, Anne, freed from her chauffeur responsibilities, had moved out of Big Brick and into the Twelve Corners apartment with Kathy. I visited every day after school, not only by myself, but with my new gang in tow.

Early in junior year, my group of McQuaid buddies had expanded exponentially. John had introduced me to Bob, an athletic boy with a prominent Adam's apple. His skin shone golden brown from the outdoor sports he played.

Bob was a member of the Camera Club, which met in the school basement. The clubhouse was a dank, windowless room containing a couple of desks and a photo lab. John and I joined Bob there between classes. It seemed like a place Jupiter would approve of.

The Club leaders included Peter, a tall, thin boy who'd grown up near John, and Tim, a shorter, studious guy with a mischievous smile. Other members included Chips, a guy with sideburns who used the word "suave" all the time and Bill, a curly-headed English major.

The seven of us began to frequent the Camera Club at lunchtime and after school. John and Bob, both natural jokesters, competed for our attention by imitating the quirks of our Jesuit teachers. We all made bets about which priests would object to our secret stash of alcohol in the developing room and which ones would join us for a shot.

When we ran out of school subjects to laugh at, we made jokes about each others' mothers and feigned indignant anger – which only made us laugh more.

On their first visit to Pal-Mac, I brought my new friends directly to HQ. They dug through my magazine collection with vigor. I had no fear they would run into my private stash – I'd moved the guy magazines into my bedroom, buried under a pile of Superman comic books at the back of my closet.

I also brought the guys to Gerard's Grocery, introducing them to Dad and Paul. Their favorite discoveries at the store included the cases of Moosehead beer, our gang's favorite drink, and the Ms. Pac-Man video game my father had recently installed. John and I immediately launched a two-player round.

Bob watched my brother, Paul, stuff cash into a small sack – the two fried eggs for The Booker. "Did anybody ever rob this place?" he asked.

I glanced up from the game board and lowered my voice. "I got held up by a guy with a ski mask and shotgun once," I said. "But the cops caught him like a month later. I had to go to court and tell what happened."

John broke in. "Yeah, and I was on the phone through the whole thing and didn't even know it was going on!"

"Holy shit!" Bob said. "Greg, whatdja do after that?"

"Well...my sister, Kathy, worked with me for a few Saturday nights, but it was a long drive out here from Rochester, so it kinda just ended up me being alone again." I continued to focus on the game as I felt embarrassment creeping into my chest.

"I did start locking the door in between each customer...I would watch out the front window to see who was coming and whether I knew 'em. If I knew 'em, I would really quick unlock the door so they wouldn't know I had it locked in the first place." I gave a short laugh. "But that got old really fast. It was too much jumping up and down. I finally just said some prayers and tried not to worry about it."

"Was it weird to see the guy in the courtroom?" John asked, waiting not-so-patiently for his turn.

I shrugged. "He was wearing a suit and there were lots of cops around. So it wasn't bad. But I will say this," I said, as Ms. Pac-Man devoured the final ghost and a tougher round prepared to start. "To this day, I get a little freaked out when I see somebody wearing a ski mask."

???

McQuaid assigned a counselor to each junior, with a requirement to meet at least one time during the school year. Mine was Father Hubert. He had a small office on the second floor above the chapel. The room resembled a storage closet that somebody had crammed a desk and chair into.

Father Hubert was a gaunt man with jet black hair. His pale skin gathered in a strange bunch beneath his chin. "He has throat cancer," Bob muttered to me as we stood in the hall one day. It was easy to believe; every time I passed my counselor's office, he held a cigarette. Clouds of smoke leaked around his door when it was closed.

I dreaded my turn in his office. I knew I had to do it once – but I avoided thinking about it.

Bob, a psychology major, went to see Father Hubert right away. Talking to a counselor was welcome territory. After his session, I asked him how it went.

"It was okay, G. We talked about a lot of things. Even masturbation."

"No way!"

"Yes, *way*. It's a normal topic from a psychology standpoint. It can help guys open up. It was okay. I like talking to him."

As I stared at my friend, I thought about the last conversation I'd had with an adult about sex – my father – two years earlier. It had been one of the most uncomfortable moments of my life.

I'd arrived home late from my Saturday night shift at Gee's. Customers had swarmed in on the warm summer night; I'd worked late with Anne to restock the beer and soda coolers.

The Booker was asleep by the time we got home, so I tucked the two fried eggs into the second drawer down and headed to the kitchen for a snack.

Drinking Dar sat at the blackened pine table, belly scrunched beneath a button-down work shirt, writing a letter on a legal pad. His bottle of scotch whiskey cast a brown shadow across the yellow page. The overhead light glared at me from the reflection on his shiny head.

Frustration flooded in. Usually by eleven o'clock on Saturdays, I had the family room to myself to watch *The Twilight Zone* and *Sherlock Holmes Mysteries*.

"Do you care if I watch some tube?" I asked.

He looked up slowly, a smile stretching across his face. "I can accept that," he said, speaking each word with careful, refined enunciation – his manner when drinking.

I snapped on the set and heated the frozen pizza I'd brought home.

Near the middle of *The Twilight Zone*, he stood up from the table, set his glass in the sink, and lumbered into the family room. "Mind if I join you?"

"No," I lied.

He sank into the couch. His breaths came in hard, wheezy puffs through the rest of the episode, a story about a plane that flew and flew, but kept ending up in weird places. When it ended, I got up and clicked the television off. I was no longer interested in more TV.

"Let's talk for a minute," he said. The pizza flopped uncomfortably in my gut. I sat back down and picked at a loose thread on the armrest to keep my hands busy.

"Gregory, your mother and I are so pleased with your progress at McQuaid. It's a fine institution. We feel it's the best curriculum we can offer you." I nodded at the Drinking Dar words, not sure where this was going. "You're getting older now and I think it's important that a father and son discuss some things." My father paused, then continued.

"It's natural that in a young man's life, he becomes curious about the opposite sex." In my stomach, the pizza turned to ice. *Did somebody find my magazines?*

"I remember when I was in high school, my head was turned by many of the gals running around the halls." His smile stretched wider, as though a pleasant memory had surfaced. I remained frozen to the seat of the easy chair.

"Around your age, a young man's body starts to develop. I assume you're familiar with the erection of the penis?" My thoughts went immediately to Adam.

"Yeah," I answered too quickly.

"Alright. And you're aware of what's involved with intercourse?"

"Yeah."

"Okay, Caboose, I just wanted to make sure that you know it's something that's reserved for the holy sacrament of marriage."

I nodded, sensing he might be wrapping up. "Yeah, you don't have to worry about me. We learned all about it from Mrs. Stirpe in sixth grade."

"Very good."

He wiped his left hand across his lips. "Well then, did you have any questions for me?"

"No."

"Okay." He struggled to hoist himself off the couch. Relief flooded me. "We're very proud of you, Greg." A sickly mixture of joy at my father's pride and angst over the conversation wrestled inside my stomach.

"Thanks," I said, standing up. "I think I'll head up to bed."

"Me too," he said. He put a hand on my shoulder. "I'm glad we had this talk."

160

I walked away from Bob toward my next class, tightness gripping my chest. I knew – with certainty – that if I entered our high school counselor's little office and closed the door, somehow, Father Hubert would distill my secrets. *That I masturbated. That I thought about boys during it. That God might be plotting my fiery destruction. A+B+C just might equal* homosexual.

I altered my regular routes through the school so I wouldn't have to pass his doorway.

???

My new gang occupied most of my time.

We each shared some classes, but all of us were in junior-year Advanced Placement English – or APE, as we liked to call it. Mr. Bradley, a lay teacher with short-cropped grey hair, taught the course. It was a hub of our school discussions. We'd gather in the Camera Club and talk about pop quizzes, overdue homework, or cliff notes.

I often chose to sit next to Bob during these discussions. A natural athlete, he played basketball, tennis, and track. I admired his ability to step into a team competition and fit in. My own attempts at team sports resurrected an image of lumbering across Saint Michael's gym-class floor, my blubber jiggling.

Although Bob wore a varsity jacket, he didn't act like a jock. He talked to me a lot, sharing his dreams of being a counselor, a drummer, a singer. We had similar musical interests, ones that most others didn't: The Carpenters, *The Sound of Music* soundtrack. Bob didn't own a Sheena album but sang along with her heartfelt ballads when I blasted them on Bufford's stereo.

I negotiated to spend alone time with him, both in school and after. I enjoyed visiting his house, sometimes lying on his bed and just talking. A poster of Heather Locklear in a skimpy bikini hung on the back of his bedroom door.

"I gotta get a Sheena poster," I said, needing him to notice my interest.

"Sheena's okay," he said, winking. "But Heather is one foxxxy lady!"

On the outside, I smiled my consent. Inside my gut, dark fear rose like bile. *Why couldn't I feel that Heather Locklear was foxy? When would my own full adolescent responsiveness finally kick in? And how long before somebody noticed that I was faking it?*

???

John and I decided to attend the spring Section V basketball semi-finals. McQuaid's team, including Bob, had advanced with each game they played.

We walked into the Rochester War Memorial, a large indoor stadium downtown, and took seats near the McQuaid basket. I spied Bob across the court. From this distance his face was unreadable, but the pensive lean of his body told me he was worried.

A row of girls chattered behind us. They'd been giggling and screeching since we took our seats. I glanced over my shoulder to see what the commotion was about.

Five girls had clumped in two rows. The one closest to me vaguely resembled Sheena. She looked about our age.

John followed my glance as the game started below. "Why don't you get her number?" he asked. "Of course, I'd give it to ya myself, but I never kiss and tell, ba-dum-bum," he joked.

I tensed. He expected me to do something. What a normal guy would do. I turned around. "Has anybody ever told you that you look like Sheena Easton?"

She smirked.

"I'm Greg, this is my friend, John."

"Hi, I'm Beth, also known as *Sheena*, and these are my friends, Dorothy, Sue, Debi, and Julie. Are you McQuaid boys? We go to Mercy."

Our Lady of Mercy was the all-girl Catholic school across town. Their student population often partnered with McQuaid for social events. I'd never been to any.

The other girls greeted us as a cheer went up from the audience. I jerked back to the game. Bob stood under the basket smiling.

"Are you a fan?" Beth asked me.

"Yeah, Bob's a friend of mine."

For the rest of the game, the girls continued to include us in their back-and-forth banter. I split my attention between them and the team on the court below.

Ninety minutes later, the final score came across the screen: East High, 61, McQuaid, 33. They'd clobbered us.

I watched Bob walk defeated from the court, my gut aching as though I'd played the game at his side. "Oh man, oh man!" John hung his head in his hands. "Let's get *outta* here," he said.

I turned toward the girls. I'd finally made a female connection. I *couldn't* let it slip away.

I was sure a regular guy would single out the hottest choice and ask for a date. I had no such discernment – they seemed pretty much the same to me. On impulse, I chose Beth. "Can I have your phone number?" I asked. *At least she reminds me of Sheena.*

"Okay," she said. She scribbled on a slip of paper and handed it to me.

"I'll call ya." I promised. As she turned her attention back to her friends, I wondered what Bob must be feeling in the locker room. John motioned for me to go.

???

As Mom and Dad's finances improved over the years, they had bought a small cottage on the eastern shore of Duck Lake, just north of Syracuse. The lake was tiny – barely one mile long – and was an hour's drive from our house. As a family, we visited a couple of times each year during the summertime heat. The Booker occasionally rented it out to family friends, but otherwise it sat, unused, for weeks at a time.

Nestled deep in the woods with few neighbors, its cabin-like feel reminded me of someplace the Hardy Boys might spend a week with their chums, working on a mystery. I decided to organized a spring trip to Duck Lake for the guys. The seven of us had visited my parents' cottage a couple of times. This would be our third Moosehead-and-Yahtzee getaway.

A week later, all seven clambered into Bufford. We made the traditional stop at my father's store for provisions, including a case of beer. Bob grabbed a six pack of ginger ale – he didn't drink alcohol.

"Do you think a case is enough?" I asked John. "Considering that I have a pint of vodka in Bufford's trunk."

He grinned. "That'll be good."

My dad stood behind the counter. "Hey guys!" he greeted my friends. Although he could be unpredictable and explosive at home, my father seemed to enjoy the camaraderie my new buddies provided. He often joked with them, or asked them about their college plans, or looked the other way when we stocked Bufford's trunk with beer. Watching him banter with my friends as though he were one of gang, I felt a twinge of bitterness in my belly.

"You guys headed to 'Moosehead Lake'?" Dad quipped, pointing to the case of bottles. We laughed.

"Just trying to support the Canadian economy," John joked back.

"Don't get in *too* much trouble. Those ladies down around Duck Lake can be pretty wild."

"Alright!" Bob cheered.

I rolled my eyes. "We'll be careful."

Back in the car, John spoke up. "You're dad's an okay guy," he said.

My face twisted as I considered the things they didn't know. "Sometimes," I responded.

We started drinking as soon as we arrived at the cottage. The gang split into a couple of groups. Some played Yahtzee, others headed onto the lake in my rubber raft. When dusk approached, we congregated around the campfire. The volume of our conversations increased with our inebriation.

The chilly night air eventually drove us back into the cottage. When the beer ran low, I began mixing Sunkist screwdrivers.

John and Bob tumbled into the rubber raft, which we'd carried into the cottage for the night. Each grabbed an oar and began to paddle. "SHARKS!" John yelled at the top of his voice.

"SHARKS!" Bob echoed. I ran for my camera and got a picture of them rowing across the carpeted floor.

Later, when we'd exhausted the alcohol supply – and our tolerance for Yahtzee – John, Bob, and I shared the pull-out couch. The other guys crashed in the cottage's two bedrooms.

As I drifted off to sleep, the room softly spinning, I dismissed the sense of disappointment that Bob and I weren't alone in the bed.

???

The guys always joked about getting together with the opposite sex, but I provided the first group connection.

Encouraged by the chatter I'd had with the Mercy girls at the basketball playoffs, I made a follow-up call to Beth. We talked for a half hour. She finished by inviting me to bring two friends and join her at a Mercy dance that Friday night. I agreed. At school the next day, I talked Bob and John into joining me. It wasn't a hard sell.

On Friday, we stood in the darkened Mercy gymnasium looking around for Beth and her friends. For the first time in his life, John had been on time when I arrived in Bufford to pick him up.

Men at Work blasted from massive speakers at either end of the space. Although kids crowded the room, very few danced. Just one group of girls at the center of the room gyrating to the beat. "At least the music is good!" I said, raising my voice to be heard. John and Bob looked around skeptically.

Beth popped out of the crowd. She wore a blue-and-white knit sweater. No frills – not resembling Sheena as much as I'd remembered. Her two friends trailed behind.

"Hi!" she said. "Hey, I'm sorry I just got here. Have you been waiting long?"

"Not that long," I said, unsure of what to do next.

"You remember Debi and Sue."

"And you know John from the basketball game. This is Bob," I said. They all shook hands. For the rest of the evening, Bob and John hung out with Debi and Sue while Beth talked with me. She covered a lot of territory: her parents, former boyfriends, musical interests. We laughed a lot, especially discovering we both liked the same Sheena Easton songs.

Before we left, I promised to call her again.

???

I couldn't avoid it any longer – I received a note on McQuaid letterhead, pushed through the slots of my locker. *Your appointment with Father Hubert is scheduled for Wednesday, April 13, at 1 p.m.*

Tuesday night, I lay on my bed listening to *Mystery Theater*, or *M.T.*, as my brother and I had nicknamed it. Paul sat in the chair at my desk. His lumpy head pitched forward every few minutes. He'd gotten up at six a.m., gone to Perkins by himself, then worked all day at Gee's.

For once, I was glad he dozed. Sometimes when we listened together, he asked me to explain the plot – and tonight I was too distracted to follow it myself. *What was I gonna say to Father Hubert tomorrow? Wasn't he trained, like a detective, to figure things out, just by the way a kid sat or how he made eye contact? I would have to go in with my Jupiter skills in high gear – one detective outwitting another.*

The slam of *Mystery Theater*'s final squeaking door brought Paul straight up in his chair. "I'm awake," he said, grinning at me.

"It's over," I said.

"But I'm awake."

"That's nice. I'm going to sleep."

"See ya on the flip side."

"Night." My brother picked up his empty ice cream bowl and closed the door behind him. I undressed and slid under the covers. As I lay in the darkness, I worked for my nightly release, but images of Father Hubert and smoke rising from his half-burned cigarette made it impossible.

The next morning flashed by. I met Bob in the Camera Club for lunch. "I have to see Father Hubert at one." I looked at him, longing for his support.

He placed his hand on my shoulder. "Don't worry, G. It's no big deal. He's a good guy. He even stopped me in the hall the other day and we talked. He reminded me how I came to him a few months ago with my pants down."

"WHAT?!"

Bob chuckled. "I told you, when we talked about masturbation. It's just an expression, G. I didn't literally pull my pants down."

"If he asks me about jerking off, I'm gettin' the hell outta there!" I said. We laughed, which helped the butterflies in my stomach find a perch.

At a minute before one, the counselor's door stood open. Light and smoke streamed out into the hall. *Jupiter always triumphed in a battle of wits,* I thought. *I'll just stay one step ahead of him and I'll be fine.* I stuck my head in. "Father?"

"Greg, come in, sit down."

He stood, balanced his smoldering cigarette on the edge of a cut-glass ashtray, then extended his right hand. I shook, feeling his cool skin under my fingers.

We sat.

He stared at me through lenses as thick as a detective's magnifying glass. "You haven't been to see me yet this year," he started.

"No, I just got the notice the other day."

I shifted in the armchair, trying to find the right pose for my legs. I settled on lifting my right ankle and resting it on my left knee. *Very masculine*, I thought.

My foot twitched. I worked to control it as Father Hubert continued.

"Some boys come see me even when they don't receive an invitation. Just to talk. Is there anything you'd like to talk about?" He picked up the cigarette, placed it between his thin lips, and leaned back in his chair.

What was he thinking?

"No, nothing," I answered too quickly. I looked him in the eyes. He did the same, his silent stare boring into my brain. I dropped my gaze.

Dammit!

Father Hubert let out a long, slow breath, smoke pouring from his mouth and nose. He opened a file on his desk – my file, presumably – and looked down for a few moments. I used the time to shift my left foot onto my right knee.

"Your grades are very good. Have you applied to any colleges yet?"

This was something I could talk about. "Well, my oldest sister, Molly, lives in Cincinnati, so I've been thinking about moving out there. We've very close. I've looked for Catholic colleges in the area and there's one, Xavier University. I'm thinking about applying there."

He took another drag on the cigarette. The tip glowed bright yellow. "Just one college? It would be wise to consider a couple of options, depending on what you'd like to study."

"Well, I'm really close to my family, so I think that's the best option for me. I know myself pretty well."

He didn't say anything. An uncomfortable silence lingered in the cloud of smoke.

"McQuaid has a large collection of college reference guides in the Guidance Office. Have you been there?"

"Yes, I looked up Xavier in one of the books. It seems like a good school."

He leaned forward. I could see the lines in his skin and thought about the cancer beneath them. I shifted my position again. "Have you discussed this with your parents?" he asked.

I'd told Mom about my plans. "Yes," I answered.

The cigarette burned down to the filter. He snubbed it into the ashtray with a series of jabs, then looked up at me. "Greg, I want you to promise me that you'll visit the Guidance Office again and try to find at least two other schools to consider. It's best if you offer yourself plenty of options."

I sensed we were nearing the end of the interview. I dropped my right foot to the floor and sat up straight. "Sure, Father, that's a reasonable approach," I said, putting on my best Jupiter tone.

He stared into my face a last time. "Is there anything else you'd like to talk about?"

"No, I think that's it." I stood up.

My counselor rose to his feet and extended his hand. "If you ever do want to talk, my door is always open."

"Thank you, Father." I shook his hand and retreated, my breath coming in staccato bursts.

In the Camera Club after school, Bob asked me how it went.

"No-prob-lay-mo," I winked, giving him a high five.

???

On impulse, I decided to give shot putt and discus throwing a chance — especially since Bob was on the track team. He ran the hurdles, his long legs gliding smoothly over the metal barriers. I enjoyed the thought of sharing a sport with him — throwing the discus and leaping hurdles fell under the overall track umbrella.

I made the cut and began the grueling task of daily after-school workouts. The effort was worth it; after practice, Bob and I often jumped into Bufford and headed to his house. We'd hang out in his room, sometimes until late in the evening. Sandwiched between his drum-set and built-in bookshelves, we'd listen to his Billy Joel albums and talk about McQuaid, or the Mercy girls, or any other subject. I'd finally say goodnight and head for the Apt – our nickname for my sisters' apartment at Twelve Corners – or sometimes just crash on a cot mattress on Bob's floor.

About two weeks into our new routine, I pulled Bufford into the circle behind McQuaid, ready to pick up Bob after track practice. He stood talking to a sandy-haired, thin boy who wore a white varsity jacket like Bob. I'd seen him running track. He was in our class, although I wasn't sure of his name.

"G., this is Roy. Mind if we give him a ride home? He lives near me." Bob said.

"Hi," I greeted Roy. He held a small bundle of clothes tucked under one arm.

"Hey," he said.

"Sure, come on, join us." I tried to sound nonchalant, but an awkward anger began to peck at my gut. *I like it when it's just Bob and me*, I thought.

Bob took the front seat, Roy climbed in back. "Do you like Sheena Easton?" I asked, plugging in a cassette.

"She's okay," he answered. His tone suggested he was being polite.

"Roy's more into The Police," Bob filled me in. He began to sing *Roxanne* in an obnoxious falsetto.

"Don't forget The Talking Heads, Bob!" Roy added from behind my seat.

"They're okay," I adopted an equally polite tone. Reaching toward the dash, I cranked up the volume on the stereo and tore out of the school's driveway. Unwelcome irritation rose in my chest, but singing along with Sheena helped me squelch it.

Sunday, May 8, 1983
It's been quite a while since I've recorded anything in my journal. I remember capturing details of "cases" in here when I was a kid. Now I only seem to read this book when I'm depressed.

The good news is that I've lost a lot of weight since starting track. But I think today I'm just feeling that everything's closing in on me. My seventeenth birthday is a week from Thursday, exams are in three weeks.

And sometimes it's kinda lonely out here at Big Brick.

???

According to a poster at the mall bookstore, *Christine*, a new novel from Stephen King, was coming soon. The afternoon it arrived, I gladly paid $16.95 for the hardcover edition. I read all afternoon on Big Brick's backyard hammock – hanging just inches above the plush carpet of grass that had been choked with prickers nine years earlier.

After dinner, I stayed at the kitchen table to enjoy the air conditioning, turning pages with one hand, munching on weighty chunks of my mother's fudge with the other.

Paul had gone to the city for an organ recital, so he wouldn't be joining me for *Mystery Theater*. When ten o'clock approached, I reluctantly abandoned the book and headed out to Headquarters and M.T.

An hour later, E.G. Marshall, the narrator of *Mystery Theater*, shut the creaky door on another "*adventure in the macabre,*" his trademark signoff line. I climbed out of the grain bin and trekked across the backyard. The driveway lights illuminated Dad's station wagon in the front lot. He'd worked the evening shift at Gee's and must have arrived home while I sat in HQ.

Inside, I stood in the hallway, considering whether to creep up the stairs unnoticed or stop in the kitchen to retrieve *Christine*. I wasn't sure whether Dad was drinking, but the desire to read in bed led me to risk an encounter.

I slid back the pocket door.

No alcohol in sight.

Sensing my father's foul mood, I made a quick sweep through the room. "Hi Dad," I said, picking up my novel and preparing to retreat.

"Hold it a minute."

I froze.

"Yeah?"

"This is your book?" he said, pointing to the slick black hardcover I had clutched to my breast.

"Yeah."

"What the *hell* do you mean, buying a book for seventeen dollars?"

I stood, my brain clawing for an answer. "I wanted it," I said, after a couple of tense seconds had passed.

"That's just great. And now you can return it."

Anger flashed through me, unexpectedly quelling the jitters that shook my gut. I had never challenged him – but this was *Stephen King*. My mother's rule *'I won't have fighting in this house!'* shouted in my head. *'Offer it up'* echoed closely behind.

I chose my words carefully, picking my way through an uncharted mine field. "I used my own money," I said. That should resolve the issue. Hardcover copies of *The Dead Zone* and *Firestarter* rested snugly on the shelf in my room. I couldn't make sense of this sudden objection. He apparently could.

"I don't care WHOSE money it was!" he exploded. "I'm not busting my ass over at that store every day to send you up there to McQuaid so you can pay seventeen dollars for one book!"

He stood and yanked the scotch whiskey bottle from the liquor cabinet, extinguishing further discussion. At least until Drinking Dar appeared, something I didn't want to hang around for.

I left the kitchen, the muscles in my arms clenching and unclenching. I paused in the doorway to glance back at my father pouring the brown liquid into a tumbler. Like a lightning bolt, a thought struck me.

He drinks to escape.

I wasn't sure exactly what he wanted to escape – my mind returned to the scene of Gram clasping her hands together as she evaluated the apartment he'd built for her, saying *'Now, if ya had it to do over again, would ya have picked that same color?'*. But, at the moment, I was too angry to care. I folded the thought into my mind for later examination as I mounted the stairs, vowing never to leave anything on the kitchen table again.

???

Junior year drew to a close much the same as previous terms. The major distinction this year was my independence – I now had my own car to visit city friends and an apartment to sleep at anytime I wanted to.

I sometimes felt guilt about not being around as much to help my mom with the Opes, but that feeling was tempered by the relief at seeing less of my father. On sober days, he continued to grouse about the everyday things that annoyed him – the size of the electric bill at Gerard's Grocery; the way Mom rotated groceries in Big Brick's refrigerator. On drinking days, he still pulled out his yellow legal pads, filling page after page with flowery letters to his relatives in California.

With my newfound freedom, I made more frequent trips to the city, sleeping at the Apt or staying overnight at Bob's. I felt sure that the gang – Bob, John, Peter, Tim, Chips, Bill, I, and now Roy – would be gathering all summer.

Bob had introduced Roy to the rest of the guys. Roy's boyish charm quickly earned him a place in the group, laughing at Bob and John's ridiculous imitations or bantering with Tim about heady stuff like physics and engineering. His dry wit made me chuckle, gently smoothing over the fact that he didn't care for Sheena's music – and that he continued to accept Bob's invitations for the drive home from school.

???

I continued my Saturday night shift at Gee's during the summer, but I found it difficult to juggle work around my growing social schedule. I spent a lot of time on the road late at night, traveling between Pal-Mac and Rochester.

Early on a Sunday morning in the middle of July, after sleeping over at Bob's, I pulled out of his driveway and headed toward Pal-Mac. Bufford's defroster struggled to remove humid dew from the windshield.

As I eased the car onto the interstate, I thought about the fun we'd had the night before. After work, Bob and I had climbed up to the city's reservoir, stared up at the stars for awhile, then raced among the trees, pretending to be soldiers in the darkness. *Maneuvers*, we called it. After that, we'd gone back to his house for ice cream and Billy Joel in his room until we finally fell asleep.

I loved spending the night at his house.

Abomination, my mind whispered.

I stepped on the gas, suddenly annoyed by the familiar guilt that spread through my body. Bob and I were friends. There was nothing wrong with the way I felt about him.

Offer it up, my brain responded.

Memories tumbled around inside my head.

Father Fredricks' speech: *Our bodies are temples of the Holy Spirit*. Adam reading in front of the Mrs. Stirpe's class: *Church Says 'No' to Gays*. The ski-masked guy at Gerard's Grocery: *Get down on the floor. NOW!*

I opened the driver's window and let the cool rush of morning air force my mind clear.

RUNAWAY PLAN: Cincinnati/Day Sixty-One (1984)

The second week of October, Molly and I had dinner at Long John Silvers restaurant. I could hardly wait to tell her about my day.

"I went to Chem class and when I walked in, the professor told me to 'write Number Three on the board.' I had no idea what he was talking about. I scrambled, tried to look it up, and finally said, 'I'm not prepared at this time to put Number Three on the. board.' "

Molly chuckled.

"I talked to the girl next to me and she explained there was a syllabus that had the homework assignments for the whole semester laid out. I hadn't even looked at it, we got it the first day and I stuck it in the book. I thought it was some stupid paper I didn't have to read.

"Then – you're not gonna believe this! – I went to my computer class today and they said that next week's class is the last one! I guess it's only a one-credit course. I had no idea it was ending and I'm kinda bummed, it's my favorite class." I finished my story and returned to my fish and chips.

Molly set down her fork and stared at me.

"What are you doing in school?" my sister asked in a low, serious voice.

I shifted in my seat, shoving another fry into my mouth.

"Whattdaya mean?"

"I mean why are you going to college? You don't know what your homework is or that a class is over? I'm just wondering what you're doing there."

She leaned forward. Her eyes drilled into my face.

"What's your purpose?"

I stopped eating.

"I don't know," I said after almost a minute's delay, which she'd allowed me without interruption. "I guess it's what I'm supposed to do."

I shifted again.

"Have you ever considered not going?" she asked, not dropping her gaze.

My mind churned. Sister Joyce at Saint Michael's, Father Hubert at McQuaid, Mom, Dad, Bob – nobody had ever asked me about whether I wanted to go to college or not. It was just one of the things everybody expected from me. Like being attracted to girls.

"You mean I don't have to?"

A light bulb went on inside my head as my mind ticked off the things I could give up. Not having to face the cranky Chem teacher with the wispy gray hair and the first-day syllabus. Not having to watch guys hook up with girls after class. Not having to fake it in front of so many people.

Another thought struck me. "But Mom and Dad already paid."

"Is the add/drop period for classes over yet?"

"I don't know; how do I find out?"

"We can call the school admissions office tomorrow. They'll know."

"How do you know all this stuff?" I asked, amazed at her street-wise wisdom.

" 'Cause I've been through it. I dropped out of college after a couple of weeks when I figured out that I didn't have a purpose. Dad was overjoyed. He got ninety percent of his money back."

Arriving home from dinner, I dug through my admissions packet. There it was, a calendar marked ADD/DROP. If I quit in the next couple of days, my parents would get eighty percent of their money back.

Relief flushed through me, followed by the confusion that had gnawed at my gut for so long. I had no idea how to make my life right. And time was too valuable to waste – Roy's accident had taught me that. I focused my thoughts on Xavier.

The strangers who sat next to me in classes and knew about syllabuses. The crowded student lot where I had to park in the farthest spot.

The disconnected loneliness I couldn't name.

I could shuck it all in the next two days.

I called Big Brick. Mom listened as I explained my plan. "Well, Honey, I really don't know—" she trailed off. I heard her cover the receiver. The evening news blared in the background.

"Darwin," her muffled words came through. "It's Greg; he wants to drop out of college." She uncovered the phone. "Here, talk to your father about it."

"What's going on?" Dad's voice boomed clear and curt over the phone. In my stomach, the tartar sauce and ketchup began to separate. He wasn't Drinking Dar, which I'd been hoping for. This would be more difficult.

I pulled out my Jupiter words. They would help.

"I'm just not really focused at this time. Molly and I have discussed it extensively and we both feel a year off is the correct strategy for me."

I knew the mention of Molly's name would aid my case. He always talked about her ability to handle things. I added my trump card. "You'll get an eighty-percent refund."

"Now just cool your jets for a minute."

It was hard to read him from Cincinnati, but he didn't sound immediately impressed with my logic. "Once you get out of that college groove, it's awful hard to get back in."

"We're going to talk with admissions tomorrow, to look at all my options. I really feel a year off will be the right thing for me right now."

"This seems like it's outta the blue! You were just showing off the campus a coupla weeks ago."

"Well, I've been thinking about it for awhile." Two hours to be exact, but I didn't need to tell him that.

I wanted out.

177

"Let me talk to Molly."

I handed the phone to my big sister. "He wants to talk to you," I whispered.

I sat in silence as she nodded and commented, defending my ability to choose and the wisdom of finding some purpose before continuing blindly through school. "Okay, Dad, we'll talk to the college tomorrow and let you know how it goes," she said and hung up the receiver.

"Well?" I asked.

"He's not happy but, ultimately, it's up to you."

I let out a cheer.

"So, you wanna have some ice cream and watch cable? I don't have homework anymore!" We both laughed and headed toward the freezer.

Chapter Eleven: *Jupiter, the Roman God of Lightning (1983 continued)*

TO PLACATE THE ugly whispers in my thoughts, I resolved to spend more time with the girls in my life. In August, I purposely scheduled time to catch up with Caroline. Although we still occasionally searched for secret rooms or hidden maps, more often we read comic books together in my bedroom or played Atari at her house. She was fourteen now.

"Did you know I really like Sheena Easton?" she asked me during a game of *Frogger*.

"No! Seriously?" I jumped at the chance to talk about my attraction to the Scottish singer.

"Yeah. It just kinda happened. I kept seeing her records over at your house. And now I really like it when she comes on the radio."

"Do you wanna borrow her albums? There's three so far and another one is due out next month."

"Sure!" She smiled up at me from her seat on the other side of the Atari equipment. The next day, I dropped off all three Sheena records.

Beth, the girl who'd kept me company at the Mercy dance, was next on my list. We talked a few more times on the phone, then got together for a late-summer lunch. She never screeched timidly about things as Gaila had done. Beth swore – and she punched or kicked me when she felt like it. After lunch, we drove around in Bufford, listening to Sheena tapes. I enjoyed her company.

???

Senior year began with a new Sheena album and a new APE teacher.

Best Kept Secret, my favorite singer's latest recording, placed a top ten hit right away with the song *Telefone*. On the flip side of the record, *Let Sleeping Dogs Lie*, a tune with a pounding beat, caught my attention. I turned up the volume every time it came on.

I longed to see Sheena in person. To stare into her penetrating eyes. To feel what other guys must feel. To halt my slide toward abomination. I checked the paper regularly for news of concerts in our area.

Father O'Malley, the senior year APE instructor, was famous around school for his film reputation. He'd actually had an onscreen role as a piano-playing priest in *The Exorcist*. I'd never seen the movie, but I admired this glitzy finger of fame stretching from Hollywood to my school. My junior APE scores earned me a coveted slot in Father O'Malley's class.

The first day, I took a seat near the back and evaluated my new teacher. He stood tall at the front of the classroom, his steel-gray hair a sharp contrast to the jet-black shirt. His long chin jutted out over the white priest's collar.

A group of students surrounded him, talking over one another. I scanned the rest of the room. The wall beside me displayed a row of framed playbills – a history of McQuaid's theatrical productions. I hadn't been to a single one, but I knew from my yearbooks that Father O'Malley was the school's director.

My eye caught the last frame just above my head. An eight-by-ten portrait of Sophia Loren. Handwriting slashed across the photo beneath her buxom chest.

I glanced toward the front of the classroom. Students continued to filter in from the hall. I had time. I stood and squinted at the flowery script.

Bill, all my love, Sophia.

All my love? I turned to see Father looking at me, a devilish grin on his face. "You like that?" he said out loud. The class' attention turned to me.

"Do you know Sophia Loren?" I asked him.

He assumed an affected arrogance. "I've been *around*." The priest winked at me, then turned back to the class. "Okay, guys, why don't you take a seat and I'll tell you about that pornographic horror flick I made out in Hollywood."

We sat.

"At the time *The Exorcist* came out as a novel, a friend of mine at the Rochester Public Library asked me to review the book for their *Books Sandwiched In* lunchtime program. It had already been on the bestseller list for six months, but it was my friend asking, so I said 'yes.' "

Not a paper rustled in the classroom. He had our full attention.

"I read the book quickly. It was very good – really grabbed me by the throat and held on! I finished the review soon after, months ahead of my debut at the library.

"I knew that William Peter Blatty, the author, had gone to Brooklyn Prep and still kept in touch with a Jesuit I knew there. I got Blatty's address and popped my review into the mail to him, expecting nothing.

"In less than a week, he wrote back – which surprised the hell out of me. He explained that he'd written the book as thanks to the Jesuits who taught him when he was younger.

"It was a pleasant-enough reply, but he took exception to my review of the Jesuits in the book. I'd written something of a scathing commentary of them, accusing them of being too *cutesy flip*."

Father O. raised an eyebrow and pursed his lips. I warmed to his animated storytelling.

"I wrote him a thank-you letter and he responded saying he'd be in Manhattan in a few weeks. Would I like to meet with him and our mutual Jesuit friend? My superior said 'okay', so off I flew.

"He was the first millionaire I'd ever met and, I have to say, before the drinks were served, I went out of my way to impress him, spouting what I was sure were true Manhattan author-style witticisms. After a bit of that, I finally stopped myself and said, 'Do you know what I've been for the last fifteen minutes?' He grinned across the table at me and said, 'Yeah. *Cutesy flip.*'

"I didn't know it at the time, but it was the start of a good friendship. Which leads me to *the call.*

"About two weeks later, the phone rang at the residence hall. It was William Blatty, asking for *moi.*" Father splayed his fingers across his chest and looked at us over half-glasses.

" 'Hello, Bill,' he said. 'Would you like to play Father Cutesy-Flip? In the movie.' I nearly dropped the phone.

"I must have said okay, because he sent me a script, I got permission, and ended up in Hollywood."

Father O'Malley leaned closer, as though to draw us into his confidence. "Which brings us to Sophia," he said, walking across the room to her picture. "After filming one night, the director and a few of us were having a drink at the local gin mill. Two of us in the cast were *actual* priests – of course the topic of celibacy came up.

"One of the guys asked if there was a woman alive who would make me break my vows. I considered it over my gin for a minute, then answered *Sophia Loren.* They loved that."

He grinned sharkishly. "It turned out one of them knew her and got a picture signed for me."

He strode back to the podium and winked. "So that's the sordid tale of Father Bill O. and Sophia."

I relished the drama of his tale. It was the best story I'd ever heard from a McQuaid teacher. And it gave me hope that I might someday meet Sheena Easton.

???

Senior year brought another change. The gang moved across the hall from the Camera Club to the Accolade Office, the school's yearbook. Tim and Peter were co-editors of the 1984 publication. I landed the copy-editor's job. Roy, Bob, John, Chips, and Bill signed up for staff positions as well – the office became a new hangout for us. We regretfully abandoned our secret alcohol stash in the photo lab, although we continued to have regular access to beer through Gee's.

???

Father O'Malley taught religion as well as APE. His course was called *Meeting the Living God*. We quickly shortened it to *Mt. God*. He laid out the curriculum on the first day.

"Welcome to my little corner of the religious world. I call it *Meeting the Living God* for a reason." He raised an eyebrow. "Think you're ready?"

Father looked over the sea of knotted neckties and tangled hair. "After an open mind, the first thing you need is a notebook, because you're going to be capturing your own thoughts." I perked up. It sounded like journaling. I was good at journaling.

"The assignments are spelled out in the course book. Your job is to complete them. My job is to give you feedback. Get it?"

I opened the course book and scanned the paragraph about belief systems and faith. The assignment was at the bottom, in italics:

How have your beliefs and faith changed since fifth grade?

What was the last major change in your personal relationship with God?

That night, before *Mystery Theater*, I grabbed a pen and began to write:

September 12, 1983

I often feel uncomfortable discussing my feelings and beliefs with anyone. I prefer to look, listen, and absorb than reveal. Yet, I don't mind writing to you. I welcome the opportunity to discuss my feelings.

I find my faith and beliefs have changed for both the good and bad since fifth grade. I recall myself as having been almost pious in those early years. I don't seem to feel that strongly about certain aspects of Catholic faith anymore. This disturbs me. Still, in many ways, I feel much closer to Jesus. He's such a wonderful friend. I like to speak out loud to Jesus, it makes Him more of a reality.

The last major change in my feelings must have been a few years ago. I love to walk at dusk in my back field with my dog and sing songs in praise of God. On one of those walks, I was confused about a lot of things. As I spoke to God, I felt His overwhelming embrace. It was like being bathed in love.

I'll leave space for a reply now.

I dropped the notebook into Father O'Malley's in-basket the next morning. Within a day, it was back on my desk. I flipped the cover open, anxious to read his reply. He'd penned one phrase below my last line:

I've got one and "Gasp!" Beautiful.

Pleased at having gained a confidante, I could hardly wait to complete the next journaling assignment.

???

Beth and I made arrangements for her and Sue to join me and Bob at Palmyra's Canaltown festival. I looked forward to spending some time with the girls. And sharing the day with Bob.

"Let's piggyback," Beth said, climbing onto my back as we watched the parade. Sue jumped onto Bob's back. We toted the girls around the town park, then headed to the local ice cream parlor to pick out cones.

I ordered a triple scoop. Although I'd slimmed down significantly during the track season, without the constant exercise, my familiar eating habits had caused my weight to creep slowly back up.

The girls took their ice cream to a picnic table nearby, while Bob and I stayed at the counter to pay.

"So, G., whattya think of Beth, huh? Seems like you two got somethin' going." He placed his hand on my shoulder and grinned broadly.

I considered his question. I liked spending time with her, talking on the phone. Maybe that's what it felt like, to want to date a girl.

He put his face close to mine. I could smell the faint aroma of sweat and hot fudge and Mennen deodorant. "Maybe," I answered conspiratorially.

His grin widened. "Good luck, man."

We stepped away from the counter and approached the girls. "Hey Beth, can I have a lick?" After a pregnant pause, I pointed to her cone.

"Here," she said, mashing the ice cream into my face.

That night, I picked up Big Brick's phone and dialed a familiar number. My stomach trembled.

Beth answered, used to late calls from me.

"I had a good time today," I said, after we exchanged greetings.

"Yeah, me too. The best part was smooshing ice cream in your face!"

I gathered a deep breath, then plunged ahead. "What do you think about us going out sometime, just you and me?"

She chuckled. My insides twisted.

"You mean like a date?"

"Yes, I mean like a date." I waited, my heart pounding.

"Took you long enough. Yes, Mr. Gerard, I would like to go out, just you and me, like a date."

We chatted for awhile longer. Finally, we said goodnight and hung up.

More than anything, I wanted to call Bob and share my news with him, but at eleven o'clock, his parents would be asleep. I decided to swing by his house first thing in the a.m. and hang out for awhile in his bedroom.

Early the next morning, I arrived at Bob's house and knocked on the porch door.

Roy answered.

My stomach flip-flopped.

Over the summer, gang events had brought Roy and me closer together. During an August trip to Duck Lake, Roy and I had wandered down to the dock by ourselves. Armed with four bottles of Moosehead, Roy positioned two in the cool water at the lakeshore; the other two he carried to the end of the dock for us to drink as we enjoyed the balmy day.

We popped the caps off our bottles and each took a long swig. "This is so damn nice," I said.

He shook his head in agreement. "Absolutely."

We talked for awhile about school, the Mercy girls, and future trips to Duck Lake. Halfway through our second beer, he glanced sideways at me, an amused smirk spreading across his face.

"Listen, Grey-g," he said, drawing out my name in a friendly way he'd concocted. "I got a proposal for you. Suppose you could go to a Police concert for free or pay a thousand dollars to see a Sheena concert. Which would you do?"

I clinked my bottle against his. "Even if it was the last thousand dollars on Earth, my friend," I said.

Our laughter echoed across the surface of the still water.

We were friends now, but I hadn't expected Roy at Bob's so early. Disappointment and guilt danced briefly through my stomach. "Hey, Roy," I said.

Bob called from the kitchen. "Hey G.!" He sat at the table, bent over a small electronic device.

"So what're you guys doing?" I stepped into the room.

"Just messin' with my walkman; it snarled a tape yesterday." He used a tiny screwdriver to ease the cassette out of the player.

"It's my Talking Heads mix," Roy offered, sitting at the table next to Bob. I took a seat at the other end.

"So what's up with you today, Greg?" Bob asked as he continued to work on the walkman.

I took a breath. "Well, nothing much...except next Friday I'm going on a date with Beth!"

They both turned to me. Bob spoke first. "Hey, man, way to go!"

"Who's Beth?" Roy asked.

"This chick Greg's been chasin' for awhile," Bob grinned, his dark eyes holding my gaze. I returned the smile. "And she is one fi-i-ine lady," he winked at Roy.

"Alright!" Roy responded.

"Yeah, we've been friends for awhile and it just kinda...happened." They chuckled.

I smirked, feeling the rush of blood to my cheeks.

"Be gentle with her," Bob joked.

???

The next Friday, Beth and I rode along the highway in Bufford, playing Sheena's *Telefone* as loudly as we could stand it. We'd just seen *The Big Chill* after a quick dinner at Pizza Hut. I exited the expressway and headed up the winding street that led into her Fairport neighborhood – a suburb between Pal-Mac and Rochester.

Dusk had fallen. Darkness shrouded the area under the maple trees that crowded her house. The popcorn and garlic bread mixed uncomfortably in my belly as angst – the same tension that had arisen on Gaila's doorstep years before – flooded through me.

The goodnight-kiss legend gnawed at my stomach like a spitty basin at my bedside.

I walked her up the sidewalk. The harsh glare from the porch light caused me to squint awkwardly as we drew near. I stopped on the cement just outside the screen door.

"Well, I guess that's goodnight," I said. The thought *can she hear my stomach churning?* flashed across my mind.

"Oh, you're not getting away that fast, Mr. Gerard," she said, drawing me close. Our lips pressed against each other.

Just like in the movies.

The movies had *not* prepared me for her tongue, which she thrust generously into my mouth. I wasn't quite sure what to do. I tickled at it with my own tongue for a little bit. That seemed to satisfy her.

We pulled apart. "Now you can say goodnight," she grinned.

I smiled broadly. I had done it!

???

Bufford's carburetor began to cough and spit, so while he was in the shop, I borrowed Dad's station wagon. It got me back and forth to school for several days, although I missed having a cassette player. Sheena wasn't featured on the radio often enough for my tastes.

On Thursday morning just before I needed to leave for school, Dad said he needed the wagon, so he swapped with me for his mammoth Chrysler. My friends laughed as I pulled the huge car into McQuaid's lot.

"Where's the parade?" John joked.

Finishing the day, I headed back to Pal-Mac, hoping to hear good news about Bufford.

"Did the garage call?" I asked Mom.

"Sorry, Honey, nothing yet." I climbed the stairs and walked into my room. Something wasn't right with my desk. I stepped closer.

A pile of empty McDonald's bags and school papers were strewn across the top. In the center sat a note. I recognized my father's sober script:

Next time you borrow my car, take your garbage with you.

– Dad.

I stood staring at the mess. One of the McDonald's bags had tipped sideways, spilling sweet and sour sauce onto my desk blotter.

My stomach boiled with feelings. Anger that he messed up my desk blotter. Guilt that I'd left garbage in his car. Embarrassment that my dad would do something so childish. Thoughts flashed by as I scraped the trash off my desk.

I think I would have remembered to clean it out when I officially gave it back to him.

He's the one who needed his car back today without any notice.

Some of this stuff isn't even mine!

That evening, Dad worked the closing shift at Gee's. I went to my bedroom early, reading. It was nearly eleven when I heard my father arrive home and toss the two fried eggs up the stairs to my mother. I turned out the light and lay in the dark, listening for the clink of bottles from the kitchen below.

The next day, the mechanic fixed Bufford's carburetor and I had my own car back. I made sure to wash and vacuum the Chrysler before I parked it back at Big Brick for Dad. Observing Mom's rule, neither one of us mentioned the trash incident.

???

During the last couple of weeks of September, Beth and I dated several times, cheering at McQuaid football games, holding hands in the movies, or sitting in her bedroom, listening Sheena. Each date ended with more kissing. I liked spending time with her, so I endured this additional task that seemed to please her.

???

In early October, I slept over at Bob's house. I gave him reports on my dating prowess. As we talked into the night, he rotated his left shoulder, grimacing.

"What's the matter?" I asked.

"I pulled somethin'. It's kinda sore."

"You want me to give you a back rub?"

"If you want, that'd be great."

He stripped to his waist and lay face down on his twin bed. I sat down next to him and began to work his knotted muscles. "Man, that feels great," he exhaled, relaxing into his pillow.

Heather Locklear stared at me from the back of his door. I repositioned, facing away from the poster.

The memory of Adam surfaced. Tension raced through my body. *Jesus, please help me not want something that is wrong*, I prayed silently. Bob's proximity raised goose bumps on my arms. I worked up and down his back, his neck, his shoulders, vigorously at first, then softly. As I wrapped up the massage, Bob began a low snore. There would be no further intimacy tonight.

I moved gingerly off his bed and lay on the mat behind the drum set, unable to sleep.

As October progressed, I spent less time with Beth and more time with Bob. We got in the habit of regular back rubs. Sometime him, sometimes me. After each massage, I quickly moved away from him, lying on the mat or putting my hands in my pockets. Anything to mask my excitement.

Beth noticed the shift in our time together. She brought it up during a couple of late-night phone chats, but I dismissed her concerns.

On a cloudless day in mid-October, I drove her home from Mercy, blasting Sheena's *Almost Over You*. Red and gold maple leaves swirled around the car in the afternoon breeze.

As we neared her neighborhood, she reached for the radio dial and turned the volume low. "Let's talk about what we're doing," she started.

I reached down and cranked the music back up.

"Let's not," I shouted over the swelling orchestra. I joined my harsh falsetto to *Almost Over You*.

Beth scowled and muted the stereo for a second time.

"NO, let's talk."

I looked over, reading anger in her glare. I didn't want to talk. I didn't want to kiss her. I wanted something else, something I wasn't going to tell her, or Bob, or anybody.

I turned the music back up.

"I don't wanna," I said, feeling shame rise like lava at my core.

"Fine," she said, turning to face the windshield. I pulled into her driveway, plowing through a pile of leaves that had gathered near the road. They crackled and flattened under the weight of Bufford's tires.

"Goodbye," she said, slamming the car door. She entered her house without looking back. I drove directly to Bob's, both to tell him what had happened and to get a back rub as consolation.

Beth and I officially broke up over the phone the next day. Surprisingly, we quickly fell back into the friendly, chatty relationship we'd had before the dating. Waves of relief flushed over me beyond anything I could articulate – even with my best Jupiter skills.

???

Father O'Malley's impish approach to subjects like faith and fornication charmed me. He answered questions without hesitation. His unobstructed honesty seemed foreign and – considering the feelings I worked to hold inside – a little dangerous.

"Why is it so important that I go into a confessional and tell my sins?" a boy near the front of the class challenged him. "If I go into the woods and talk to God about what I've done wrong, isn't He listening?"

"Of course He is!" Father leaned across his large wooden podium and winked at him. "But when was the last time you *did it*?"

None of us replied.

Another day, we discussed the Church's history of social conscience. "If the Catholic Church is supposed to serve the lowest of the low, it seems lame that some churches have big ornate gold chalices and expensive stuff like that," a guy three rows from me pointed out.

Father O. looked him directly in the eye as I waited for the answer.

"I couldn't agree more!" our teacher said emphatically.

No topic was taboo.

Father lectured during one religion class about the nature of God. Our priest-teacher sat perched on the edge of his table, somehow maintaining balance as he tilted toward us, his arms folded tightly across a steel-gray sweater.

"Some people seem to think of God as one of the Roman myths – a judgmental father figure sitting on a throne, tossing out lightning bolts from on high – harsh, critical, without capacity for compassion or discernment."

My body stiffened. All other sounds dimmed except Father O'Malley's voice. His words slowed with precision.

"If God is truly like that, *I pray that I never see His face.*"

I'd gotten used to his offbeat delivery, but my eyes threatened to swell from their sockets. *Wasn't it an unforgivable sin, to say you didn't want to meet God?*

My stomach churned as I mentally sifted the statement. *'If God is truly like that, I pray that I never see His face.'*

Father O.'s pronouncement bore its way into my brain.

Had I spent the last four years waiting around for a lightning bolt to strike me down? Was that the end point of the almost-constant shame I felt? My head spun with what I'd learned over the years:

If man lies with a man, both of them shall be put to death for their abominable deed—

God is love—

The Lord rained burning sulphur and destroyed them and the whole valley—

Offer it up—

Father O'Malley had proposed an alternative to offering it up, something I hadn't dared to consider. *If God is truly like that, I pray that I never see His face.* Was his approach to God unforgivable?

He was a Jesuit, holy and wise. I trusted him. My Jupiter-logic fought to make sense of it.

No, not unforgivable, I concluded. *It was more honesty.* The torrent in my belly and mind eased off. God *had* to respect honesty. Maybe I could do the same.

Father O'Malley's boldness clung to me like burrs from the field behind the barn. I didn't dare talk about the confusion over my feelings for Bob – but something else had been festering inside me for almost as long. That night, I picked up my Mt. God notebook and began to write, without having an assignment:

October 17, 1983

I was going to start this page with something dramatic, like "Do you think it's bad to hate your father?" but I decided to write it this way, so that I don't start it that way, yet achieve the same effect. I guess I don't really hate him, but it's a far cry from the kind of relationship I want to have with my sons.

I am probably writing this to hear myself say it, but I like having you around to read it.

My oldest sister told me that when I was four, he yelled at me at the dinner table, and I leaned over to my mother and whispered, "I don't like that man down there." I think that attitude has persisted for all of my seventeen years.

He's not a bit like me, he has an irrational temper and is cranky. Although I've felt cheated for years for having to learn how to shave, how to date, etc. on my own, I never minded too much, because it would be worse if he were involved in everything.

Well here it is my senior year, and I'm beginning to notice the gap. I don't even know this 63-year-old man, much less like him. I think I deal with it so well because I have always had my brothers, sisters, and mother to guide me. We're a very close-knit family, in spite of him. It is sad, because I sense he wants to have a real swell loving family, but he doesn't seem to know how. It makes me pity him.

I paused for a moment, thinking about the night Dad and I had argued about the purchase of *Christine*. I bent over the notebook and continued to write.

I know he's screwed up himself. His own dad left when he was little. I think his mom (my Gram – I liked her a lot!) was critical of him. He drinks a lot, and is deadly mellow when he drinks. I think I prefer him drunk because I can ignore him and he isn't yelling or griping.

I'm beginning to wonder if it's my attitude that is holding back a relationship. He hardly knows anything about my life. I have already said I am moving to Cincinnati next year to live with my sister, but he has ignored or forgotten that.

This is my last year at home. I don't know if I want to leave with things as they stand. I'd be content, I suppose, but sad about the whole thing.

I dropped the notebook onto Father O.'s podium the next morning, still riding the wave of courage he'd inspired. Throughout the day, my insides rumbled as I imagined him reading my written thoughts. I ate a hearty lunch and supper.

When I came to class in the a.m., my Mt. God notebook lay on my desk.

I flipped to the latest entry. As was his habit, Father O'Malley had written short comments throughout the text.

It makes me pity him, I'd written.

That's a start, Greg, he'd scribbled in reply.

I'm beginning to wonder if it's my attitude that is holding back a relationship.

His straightforward response: *It certainly helps.*

His comments were my sole focus. Next to my last paragraph, he'd written more than on any other entry:

Don't leave with things as they stand. Give it at least <u>one</u> honest try, Greg. Find some excuse – or ask him flat out – to go for a ride or to McDonalds (on <u>you</u>). Ask him, flat out, what you mean to him. Let <u>him</u> talk – and talk and talk.

I closed the book as my stomach squeezed so tight it ceased all function.

???

Bob and I lay in his bedroom in the dark after he'd turned out the light on his nightstand. Under the protection of darkness, I considered telling him what I'd written about Dad in my Mt. God notebook. And how scared I was by Father O'Malley's reply.

He might give me a hug. It might go on from there.

I turned over, uncomfortable with the mix of passion and confusion that surged below my belt.

Bob heard my movement. "G.," he said softly. "You still awake?"

"Yeah."

I turned my head toward his voice, glad that the light was out, glad that I was on the floor behind the drums, my desire shrouded.

"Would you be upset if I started dating Beth?"

My mind rocketed. I guess I'd seen this coming. The three of us had been spending a lot of time together. I'd noticed the way he held the car door for her. The way he wrestled with her on the floor of his family room.

The way I wanted to be with him.

I choked up. "Not at all, I'd be so happy for you both." I meant it, feeling my connection with him deepen through the darkness. I reveled in the moment.

"Thanks," he whispered and turned over in his bed.

I lay awake on the floor for a long time.

Bob and Beth started dating in November. She and I continued to talk on the phone and hang out at her house – when she wasn't with Bob.

The three of us continued gathering for events. Despite the strong friendships in every direction, I soon realized that the dynamics had shifted. Beth now shared something with Bob that I couldn't.

I'd watch them cuddle at football games, at movies, in the back seat of Bufford. Seeing his arm around her shoulders – seeing him bury his face in her hair – caused something to ache deep inside my gut, like a spiky rodent clawing its way through my intestines toward my heart.

I successfully quelled the feeling with popcorn, or chocolate almond custard, or any other food in available supply.

???

Feeling the loss of Bob's exclusive attention, I sought out alternatives, like visiting Headquarters or hanging out with the rest of the gang. Spending so much time in the city, my routine now rarely included things I'd enjoyed so much just a year or two before: listening to M.T., installing defenses, or preparing for cases.

Using the phone at the apartment, I called around. John, Roy, Tim, and Chips were up for a trip to Pal-Mac. We'd just received our senior mugs – beer steins with the McQuaid logo – so we decided to christen them in Headquarters.

Arriving at Big Brick, we found Paul sitting alone at the kitchen table, scooping ice cream into a bowl with slow, deliberate movements. Something about the kitchen-light's glow – reflecting off the scars that covered his skull – leached a healthy serving of guilt into my gut. It had been months since I'd shared ice cream and *Mystery Theater* with my brother. Or paid him much attention at all.

I tried to shake off the feeling with conversation. "Gentlemen, you know my bro."

"Hey Paul," John said. The other guys waved.

"Hi Fellas!" he answered, then held up the metal scoop. "Want some ice cream?"

"We're actually going for something with a little more kick," I said, holding up my mug.

"I *see*," he said, smirking. "Don't let me get in the way of a man and his beer."

In the barn, I climbed the ladder to HQ. Tim handed up a few six packs of Moosehead, then followed me up.

"You still got your magazine collection?" John asked, climbing through the ceiling entrance.

"Yeah." I pointed to the large stack. After some brew and a game of Yahtzee, we sifted through the magazines. Chips laughed, turning one sideways, extending the centerfold.

It pictured a woman with huge breasts standing naked in front of a motorcycle. *Gina*, the name in the corner of the poster read.

"Hi, Gina," he said to the picture. I tore it from the magazine and nailed it to the grain bin wall.

She watched over us as we toasted our mugs, our teachers, our school, and our manhood. My head began to spin.

"These are the good times," Roy smiled, refilling each of our steins. "Grey-g, if you just had some Police albums, this would be perfect."

I rolled my eyes. "What, Sheena's not good enough for ya?"

He raised his mug. "To Sheena!" he yelled.

"SHEENA!" we all cheered in response.

The party continued for a long while as we finished off the alcohol supply. I had consumed more than my share.

"I guess we better call it a night. Bye, Gina," I slurred, climbing past the poster. My friends led me stumbling into the house.

"I love you guys," I said. I really meant it – and through the beer haze, my stomach didn't even murmur at the honesty.

"But will you respect us in the morning?" John joked. Everybody laughed.

In the house, no one was awake. John and Tim dumped me into my bed, then the four of them returned to the city.

???

On a Tuesday night in December, I lay sprawled across Beth's bed, talking to my former girlfriend. I'd managed to book some alone time without Bob. It was late, almost ten. I didn't have a long drive to the Apt, so I lingered.

We talked – about music, about school, about her dating Bob.

I grew quiet.

"What's the matter? Does that bother you? I don't want this to hurt our friendship," she said.

"No, it doesn't bother me," I answered. "I love you. I want you to be happy. I love Bob, too."

I paused, as emotions roiled inside my chest. Perhaps inspired by my Mt. God journaling, for once, the secret stirrings inside me sought expression.

I looked across at her, then down. *I can trust Beth.*

"I think I'm in love with Bob."

She shifted closer to me on the bed and smiled. "That's sweet. You mean you love him, I know you two are close."

I worked to make her understand, my stomach ratcheting tight. "No, it's *really* strong. I think I'm in love with him."

She chuckled. "Greg, you're a sweet guy. It's okay that you love Bob. You're just confusing yourself. It's not like you're lusting after his body."

I didn't respond.

She didn't seem to notice as she chattered on about my sensitivity.

???

Christmas fell on a Sunday. I trudged through the snow drifts that had gathered across the end of Big Brick's driveway and crossed the street for a review of Caroline's gifts.

Her mom gave me a cup of eggnog as we sat amidst the piles of wrapping paper. "I know you're not quite old enough for this yet," she said, pouring a shot of rum into my drink, "but it's Christmas."

Caroline and I talked for awhile. She showed off her ski equipment and clothes, then pulled out a square, flat object. "Look what I got!" she said excitedly.

The new Sheena Easton LP. We talked about the cover photo and the different songs, rating which ones were danceable, which ones were romantic. "We *gotta* go see Sheena sometime," I said. "We just *gotta*."

"Yeah."

Lying back on the carpet under the tree, I watched her stack her gifts into a pile separate from her parents. *She's a good friend*, I thought. *I really love her and Beth. Is that all there is to it? Is that what I've been waiting for all these years?*

We played a round of *Frogger* on Atari before I headed out into newly falling snow.

???

Tuesday, December 27, 1983

It was a nice Christmas this year. We've got the whole week off.

I haven't done anything about Father O'Malley's advice to take Dad out yet. I guess I just don't want to deal with it.

I've gotten very close to all my wonderful friends lately.

I've been afraid I might be gay for about four years – this year, through getting closer to Beth, Caroline, and the other Mercy girls, I've finally come out of it.

RUNAWAY PLAN: Cincinnati/Day Sixty-Two (1984)

The next day, I worked fast and hard to unravel the threads of the college noose I'd willingly tied. I discovered one final hurdle. The admissions office required that I meet with a counselor to get permission to drop. An image of thick smoke and translucent glasses rose in my mind. I shoved it aside.

Xavier's freshman counselor was Father Keneally. I hadn't met with him yet. I made an emergency appointment for that evening.

Molly met me for the counseling appointment. She dressed in her chocolate-colored business suit, the same one she wore to important meetings at the nursing home. We parked in the visitor lot near the office buildings and walked across the leaf-strewn grass.

Darkness fell earlier each day and the evening sun lent an eerie, muddy grayness to the stone buildings. Molly stepped onto the concrete threshold and caught her heel, stumbling forward. We started laughing. The seriousness of the impending meeting fueled our desire to break the tension.

Father Keneally's office was just off the main hallway. His light seemed the only glow in the dimly-lit building. I peeked in before knocking. A tall man with graying temples sat behind an impressive desk. He wore the traditional priest garb; the placard on his desk confirmed his name.

I knocked lightly.

"Good evening, Father," Molly and I spoke over each other. A quick glance at her made me realize that she was on the verge of busting up. I looked away. We had to hold it together until this was over.

"I'm Greg Gerard," I said, extending my hand.

He took it. "Welcome, son. And are you Greg's—?"

"I'm Molly, Greg's older sister." They shook hands.

"It's a pleasure to meet you both. Please, be seated." He gestured to the solid wooden armchairs facing his desk.

We sat.

"You mentioned to my secretary that you needed a drop slip signed."

"Several, actually. I'm interested in taking a hiatus from college right now, Father." I didn't dare look at Molly. I could feel the dark burn in my gut wanting to burst out.

"Gregory," he lowered his voice and opened a file folder on his desktop. My file. "Have you thought about this? You come to us with an excellent record from McQuaid. Now, many times, there's an adjustment period involved in transitioning to college."

"I have considered it, Father, I feel this is the right course for me right now. I'm not sure exactly why I'm here and I just feel it would be better for me to take a year off." I leaned toward him and lowered my voice. "I don't have a purpose."

He didn't appear impressed with my logic. "Have you discussed this with your parents?"

Molly spoke up, putting on her own version of Drinking Dar. "Greg and I have had quite a few discussions about this, both with our parents and with each other. I've observed that he seems to lack a direction or focus to really apply himself right now in college."

Jupiter couldn't have said it better.

"And your parents are in agreement?"

"They're not overly pleased, but they have a lot of faith in Greg's judgment. Now that they're over the initial shock, I think they've come around."

Father Keneally leaned forward, his hands spread flat on his desk. "It's not unusual for a young man to lack some direction at this time in his life. In my experience, embracing a little discipline will help you find that focus. It's very difficult to make the break and then come back. Why don't you think about putting your shoulder to the wheel, you know, bite the bullet and apply yourself?"

I settled into my Jupiter tone.

"No, Father, I know myself pretty well and I'm clear this is the correct course of action for me right now."

I wanted out of there, away from this holy man's "shoulder-to-the-wheel speech," out of this stony school, away from the crushing disconnect I couldn't seem to solve.

"How about keeping just one course? That will ease up your schedule and help you keep your feet wet. Keep your shoulder to the wheel—" he looked directly at me. I knew we were moving in the right direction, so I answered quickly.

"Okay, I'll keep French, I've been enjoying that course." I'd actually only learned two phrases – how to say my name and how to ask directions to the bakery – but I wasn't telling him that. I was too close to getting what I wanted.

He smiled at the compromise.

Father Keneally pulled a thick black pen from its holster on his desktop and began signing the slips I needed. "Thank you, Father."

I let out some of the breath that had built to a tense pressure inside my chest.

"My door is always open," he finished, standing to shake both our hands.

We barely made it out the front door before we began hooting. By the time we reached the car, tears dribbled down my face. My gut convulsed. "All—I—could—think—of," I gasped between breaths, "was—that he and Drinking Dar could throw back a couple of scotches—and talk about—my excellent Catholic education!"

I broke off as Molly keeled over sideways, her face contorting with the image of our father and the Xavier "father" engaged in a lengthy, endlessly circular conversation.

"All I could think," she managed to giggle out, "—while he was talking—was that—we had parked—at our own risk—and we should run like hell for the door!"

We cackled and howled for several minutes, laughing and crying in the Xavier administration parking lot as hysterical relief washed out of me in torrents.

The next morning, I showed up early for French. Before class began, I quietly asked the teacher to sign the drop slip. She did it with minimal questions.

Chapter Twelve: And Then You Die (1984)

DURING FEBRUARY, in APE class, we read *Waiting for Godot*, the story of two characters bored, literally, to death. To break the monotony, they wanted to hang themselves. Father O. explained.

"Do you know why they keep talking about hanging themselves? The kick for them is that when a man is strangled, he gets an erection – as a little bonus." He sat on the edge of his table and crossed his legs. "Or a *big* bonus."

The class laughed, then fell silent, as we did whenever Father O'Malley talked to us man-to-man. "There was a portrait of Jesus on the cross painted a few years ago. It was created when realism was hot, capturing the suffering of our God and the brutality of the Crucifixion. A cross is a bloody, hellish mess, but it does its killing by strangulation. You hang there and try to lift yourself up, to get your next breath. And your next. And your next. Until you can't anymore."

Father O'Malley stared at us from his perch on the table, his face deadly serious. "Well, in this portrait, the artist tried to grab the true horror of the scene. He painted Jesus hanging in death, with the scars, with the blood – *and with an erection*. What a flap *that* caused!"

I didn't breathe.

"Fundamentalists rallied around it as a desecration. What they forget, when they get so excited about Jesus the God, is Jesus the Man. He was *divine* and He was *human*."

I felt my cheeks warm slightly, as my mind cautiously reviewed the image. I felt an odd sense of comfort. Jesus was male. My Lord had an ill-timed hard-on, maybe feeling embarrassment or shame.

A struggle I could share.

Later the same month, we deconstructed a short story – which included a father-son talk about masturbation. "You know, about masturbation," Father O. looked across his half-glasses, a Grinch-like smirk dividing his face. Each student assumed a casual, disinterested expression.

"You've heard that it's a sin. Or that you'll go blind." He fluttered his eyelids playfully. "What you'll learn when you get some years *under your belt*," he leaned forward and grasped both sides of the wooden podium, "is that *it's just so damn lonely.*"

I maintained my indifferent exterior, but inside, my mind spun. What a difference from the speech Father Fredricks had delivered four years before! Father O'Malley could take a subject that plagued me into unsettled secrecy and talk about it like we were chatting over lunch.

I shifted in my chair as he continued the lesson. I wasn't ready to participate in the discussion, but I drank in his words.

In the subsequent weeks, I thought about what Father O. had said about masturbation. I wasn't sure I agreed. It was a highlight of my day and, in my mind, I was never alone.

???

Molly called from Cincinnati. As usual, I filled her in on Big Brick happenings and my high school relationships. I cautiously edited what I shared about Bob.

We moved on to plans for my arrival that August. "I'm looking around at apartments," she said. "I was thinking we'll need a bigger place when you come out for college."

"That sounds great," I replied, excitement and anxiety vying for purchase on the walls of my stomach.

???

In April, the McQuaid hockey team earned a tournament tour through Europe. The schedule overlapped with Spring Break, so the school made a unique and popular decision, granting all students an extra week off. I counted the calendar days we wouldn't have to be in school: seventeen.

Bob's and Roy's families planned a joint trip to Myrtle Beach and extended the invitation to John and me. We worked out the travel details. Bob, John, and I would drive in Bufford. Roy's parents wanted him with the family, so he was not allowed to join us in my car. We were disappointed, but his parents stood firm.

On a Sunday afternoon, both sets of parents, along with Bob's and Roy's little sisters – and Roy – all pulled out of town. The rest of us would leave the next day.

That night, John and I slept over at Bob's house. As I lay on the mat in the darkness of Bob's room, I smiled, listening to his soft, sleepy snoring. I loved Beth – and I was happy that they'd found each other – but I felt a pleasant satisfaction to have him to myself for a whole week. No Beth.

John, Bob, and I left early the following morning. We made the automatic detour to Gerard's Grocery. Arriving before Paul opened the doors, I used my key to let us in. We filled up on gas and snacks. On a whim, I tossed a steno notebook into the bag. It could be a handy record of our journey.

Several states later, I pulled out the notebook and began to write:

Monday, April 23, 1984
G: 5:25 p.m. – it's been 12 hours in the car – we are all still speaking – getting along quite well, actually.
Bobby is reading.
Johnny is cruising at 69 (Ar Ar).
I am remaining diligently faithful to the annals (sp?) of history here in the death seat.
We have played so far:
- *1 Grandma went to the Market (with an attempted Gramdma went to the Porn Shop)*
- *2 Alphabet searches (Johnny and Greg, consecutive victors)*
Nothing much else to report at this time.

The guys added their own entries over the next few hours. John noted the French-tickler condoms for sale at a Texaco station and Bob kept a log of all the hot chicks he saw along the route. We finally pulled into Myrtle Beach at eleven thirty p.m. – we'd been on the road seventeen hours. We found Roy and explored the hotel before crashing for the night.

The next morning, we left the younger sisters behind and roamed the beach. It was cloudy, so we didn't spend any time on the sand, but the hotel's Jacuzzi and sauna were great substitutes. Bob pointed out females at every turn, noting the ones he thought were the hottest.

Roy kept an eye out for places we could buy Moosehead. He'd just turned eighteen, the legal drinking age, which helped us acquire beer in the absence of Gerard's Grocery.

The next days were filled with girl-watching and sunshine. Beach-side cabanas lined both sides of the outdoor pool. We watched which rooms cute girls came out of and made jokes about nocturnal visits.

I noticed how the guys made their choices without thought: a girl near the bar in a bikini was "a dog," but the one in a blue suit tanning by the pool was "a babe." I mimicked their behavior as best I could, selecting girls with blonde hair or large breasts as worthy of our masculine attention.

That night, I recorded our adventures in the trip journal.

April 26, 1984

G. here again. We were in the steam room today and 3 babes (absolutely sweet) entered, looking for some guy named Kevin. We were more than happy to assist them. We walked with them for a bit. They entered Room 151.

Later, we called Room 151 and Roy asked for Kevin, to get us an in. No luck.

Our last day in town, we rented two golf carts and shot nine holes. I enjoyed riding with Bob. It was the first time we'd been alone all week. Roy piloted the other cart, John at his side.

After the last hole, Bob added up the scores. "Of course, I shot the best with a 53," he grinned at us, "Roy got a 63, Johnny's in for 64, and Greg, you're last with a bicentennial 76."

John grabbed the scorecard with mock seriousness. "Lemme see that, let's just check those numbers, ahh—"

Roy pulled their cart close.

"I can see by this sheet that—" he paused for dramatic emphasis, "—that we'll beat your asses back to the clubhouse!" He jumped onto the cart and they sped down the two-mile path. Bob and I chased them, temporarily taking the lead, but Roy and John pulled into the parking lot first.

After some Jupiter-worthy negotiation on Roy's part, his parents agreed to let him join us in Bufford for the return trip. The next afternoon, we packed the car and headed home. We spread the trip over two days, heading first for my brother Mike's place in Virginia. I hadn't seen him since Christmas, but I'd written him. He was expecting us.

Out of the Air Force, he lived by himself in a trailer near Virginia Beach. He took classes at the community college to earn a business degree.

We got lost somewhere in North Carolina. It was nearly eleven by the time we pounded on my brother's door. He finally answered, wearing shorts and flip flops, blinking drowsily. We brought our gear into the living room of his trailer.

"You guys want to go to The Rebel for a beer?" Mike asked us. The Rebel, a one-story clapboard bar and grill, bordered Mike's park. Although Roy and Mike were the only legal-aged drinkers, we quickly agreed, tramping across the gravel parking lot. A few motorcycles sat near the entrance.

At the door, no one asked us for ID.

It was good to see my brother with my friends in tow. On his infrequent visits to Pal-Mac, he often busied himself with dates –

we rarely talked. Here at The Rebel, I felt on even ground. A guys' night out.

He caught us up on life after the Air Force as he poured a round from a pitcher of beer. Bob drank ginger ale. We told my brother about our escapades in Myrtle Beach, paying special emphasis to the many beautiful women in town.

"You guys wanna go to The Foxy Cat?" Mike asked as he filled our beer mugs a third time. "It's the best strip club in town."

"Sure!" Bob said, nearly tipping over his glass of soda.

My stomach tensed. I'd never been to a place like that before. The thought of the faking I'd have to do raced through my intestines. In a strip club, I might be *figured out*.

"It's kinda late—and we do have a long drive tomorrow," I said, trying to mask angst with concern.

"Get a life," John said, slapping me on the back.

"WATCH THE SUNBURN!" I yelled too loudly, then felt my cheeks warm as the guys laughed.

"Or we can stay here and drink," Mike offered, looking at me.

"That's probably best. It's late," I reiterated with Jupiter-certainty, trying not to arouse my brother's – or my friends' – suspicions.

"So, Mike, have you seen Greg's porno collection out in Headquarters?" John asked.

My brother laughed. "I've been to Headquarters, but there wasn't any porn there."

"I guess you haven't been there lately!" John laughed, along with Roy and Bob. I felt my cheeks flush.

"I see how it is," Mike said, grinning sharkishly.

In spite of my embarrassment, I felt a surge of satisfaction. I sensed my brother's approval. Mike continued. "Ya know, I'm the one who showed him where that grain bin was. After he lost a bet to me for twenty dollars. Which," he added, "you never did pay me for."

"You said I didn't have to!" I said, spilling a little of my beer on the table. My friends laughed again.

"Let's hear this one," John encouraged.

"Well, when we were little, I bet Greg that there was a secret room in the barn," my brother said. "He was only seven or something. I'd found those grain bins the day before. Greg didn't know anything about it."

I interrupted. "Yeah, so of course, I took the bet! It *was* a cool secret room, though. But you said I didn't have to pay," I repeated.

He laughed. "No, you don't have to pay. I just wanted to show you a secret. I knew you'd like it. You were such a little detective back in those days."

"I don't know, I don't know, it sounds like Greg welched on the bet." John never missed an opportunity to razz me. Especially when he was drinking. "What would Father O'Malley say about not living up to your responsibilities?"

Roy chuckled as I reached across the table and smacked John across the side of his head.

Bob spoke up. "Now, G., let's not resort to violence." He winked at John. "Taking responsibility for your past actions can be a first step in defining your future character," he said, poking at my ribs.

"HE SAID I DIDN'T HAVE TO PAY!" I reiterated, not enjoying that Bob aligned with John in the joke against me. I took a swig of beer and stared at them. "Besides, my future character's just fine, thank you very much."

My friends and brother laughed.

The next morning, we set out by eight. Bob took over the trip journal, adding observations about my driving, John's navigating, and Roy's whistling. Other than concerns about Bufford's radiator, which threatened to boil over every time we climbed a Pennsylvania hill, the trip was uneventful. We reached Rochester late Saturday evening. I dropped John off, then Roy, pulling last into Bob's driveway.

"We didn't really get much alone time this trip," I said as he yanked his satchel from the trunk.

"G., give it a rest, we just spent five days together!"

I read his tone and shut my mouth. *A normal guy would be happy with the five days.*

"See ya in school," he said, walking around the other side of the car.

"See ya," I said, stepping into Bufford.

He didn't offer to hug me goodbye, I noted.

???

High-school graduations, like first communions, were a proud tradition in my family. At both, we attended a ceremony, watched a procession, then filled up on food afterwards.

I'd watched each of my brothers and sisters toss their square hat into the air, tassel streaming like a kite string. I longed to hang my own tassel from Bufford's rear-view mirror as Paul, Molly, Kathy, Mike, and Anne had done before me.

I had already selected Xavier University as my Cincinnati college destination. At the end of the summer, I'd be packing my car and moving west. Away from my family. Away from my friends. Graduation was the first step on that journey. A mix of excitement and fear began to settle over my days.

McQuaid's graduation was scheduled for June sixth at the Eastman Theater, a guilded auditorium in downtown Rochester. I knew from old yearbooks that seniors wore tuxes for their photos, but when I received the instruction package for the Eastman ceremony, I realized we wouldn't have gowns. No square hat. No tassel.

I complained to Bob as we tried on our jackets for a final fitting. After a week away from each other post-Myrtle Beach, we'd returned to our routine of backrubs and overnights. I felt more relieved than I knew how to express.

"Why do we have to wear these stupid tuxes?" I asked him.

Bob pulled on his white tuxedo coat. "I don't know...I think they're kinda classy, G."

My eyes lingered as he examined his reflection in the three-way mirror. The sharp cut of his jacket. The dark curl of his hair over the edge of his collar. I longed to run my fingers through his locks, but a force as powerful as Armageddon riveted my arm to my side.

The next night, we sat on the stage of the theater. I peered into the darkened auditorium, trying to spot my family. With the lights bright in my face, it was impossible.

"*Gregory Gerard*," the MC announced over the loudspeaker. I rose and walked toward our principal. He was a tall, older Jesuit priest dressed in a long black gown. I'd rarely had occasion to visit him in my four years at McQuaid. He smiled and shook my hand warmly.

"Congratulations," he said, handing me my diploma. A brief round of clapping burst out, along with a high, whooping cheer. *That's probably Anne or Beth*, I thought, unable to see beyond the edge of the stage. I returned to my chair, a Cheshire-Cat grin stretching the limits of my jaw.

When the ceremony finished, I strode up the backstage corridor to greet Mom, Dad, Paul, Anne, and Kathy.

"Here comes the star of the class!" Dad said, shaking my hand. "Now you can show 'em how it's done out in Cincinnati." My chest swelled with my father's pride. It felt confusing – and good. I let the emotion grope around inside me, searching for a home.

Anne smiled. "Hey, ya know, congrats." Paul, Kathy, and my mom beamed.

"I can't believe it's all over!" I looked around at the sea of tuxes. Everybody gathered with family in front of the theater.

"Let's stop somewhere for dinner, then you can go join your friends after that," Mom said, maintaining her Booker role.

"Okay, great!" I agreed.

The gang eventually gathered in a tight circle. John, Chips, Bill, Peter, Roy, Tim, Bob, and me. Our relatives and the Mercy girls chatted amiably with each other.

I wanted a quiet moment with Bob. He was talking to his sister, Carol, and Roy's sister, Alison. I waited until I caught his eye. "Congratulations, G." His arms encircled me and squeezed tight.

"Right back at ya, man." I pulled away quickly, cautious not to hug him too long in front of everybody.

Father O'Malley stood on the sidewalk; a line of young men waited to see him. "Hold on a sec," I said to my family, stepping into line. It took a few minutes to reach my teacher/mentor.

His gaze locked my own and, without speaking, he gathered me into a hug. As we embraced, he spoke one word into my left ear.

"*Think*."

More emotions tumbled inside me, threatening to leak onto my face. My eyes sought the dirty pavement, the tires of a parked car, the dull shine of his priest shoes – anything to break the intensity of the moment.

Father O. moved on to the next boy in line. I returned to my own circle, wondering if I'd made him proud.

???

One topic had been burning in my gut since October. Something I couldn't put off much longer. I was leaving for Cincinnati in a month and I'd never acted on Father O' Malley's advice from my Mt. God notebook.

I didn't want to – but I knew it was the right thing to do. God would be pleased.

An early July morning, I summoned the feeling of pride my dad had expressed at graduation, gathered my courage, and dialed the store. My father answered. I kept my words short, saying I wanted to talk about something, could we go to lunch?

He agreed without asking any questions. We made plans to meet at the Perkins in Fairport.

By the time I pulled Bufford into the parking lot, Dad's 1969 Chrysler 300 – his latest vehicle purchase – already crowded a space. I made the slow march across the hot tar and eased the door open. A blast of air conditioning hit me.

I spied him, my overweight, balding father, sitting in the first booth, facing away from me. He was hard to miss in his bright yellow button-down shirt with *Gerard's Grocery* printed on a white label over the pocket. An indefinable emotion ground through my chest, circling my heart. I stood for a moment, willing it to pass.

I slid into the seat across from him. "So you beat me here."

"Yeah, I stopped to look at a used freezer and we wrapped up pretty quickly. It was a piece o' junk."

I buried my face in the menu. It bought me a couple of minutes to negotiate with the butterflies that shredded my stomach.

The waitress came and took our order. I asked for a Big Fritz. Dad ordered two eggs and toast. Underneath the table, my gut alternately clenched and unclenched. I prayed the food would arrive quickly.

"So, what's up, Caboose?" He used the nickname I hadn't heard in a very long time.

I cleared my throat and took a big gulp of water.

"Well – I just thought I'll be heading off to college in a month – and I was thinking – well – it seems like we've never really talked and I didn't want to leave without doing that. I mean I don't feel like I even know you that well."

He looked down. The fingers on his left hand fluttered against the table as though he were playing chords on his piano.

He glanced over at me. "I'm not quite sure where this is coming from, Greg. I mean, we've been working side-by-side for years. Seems like we've never had any particular problem."

I continued in a rush, gaining momentum. It was like vomiting.

"It's just that I'm your son and I love you and I didn't want to leave without trying to talk."

I had said it!

I had followed Father O.'s advice.

Like being in the confessional, even if I received a weighty penance, the relief of getting through the speech was worth it.

His expression stretched thin.

215

"Well, I'm your father and I love you too. I think we've done okay, I mean, you've worked at the store for years and it seems like we've gotten along."

He tilted his head slightly to the right while he spoke. His bushy eyebrows sloped like caterpillars making a trek down his brow.

"I know Paul gets the chance to be there everyday, so I see more of him and Mike, well, he never wanted to spend any time at the store, but you've been a part of the show all along."

I wasn't sure what to say next. Father O'Malley had only scripted the opening scene. Relief began to suffocate under other emotions that fought to register on my face. I didn't want to cry in front of him – and I sensed his comfort level nearing its own maximum.

"It's okay. I guess I just wanted to say that before I headed out of town. I'm looking forward to it. I think it'll be good giving Molly some companionship," I segued to a more neutral topic.

"Yeah, she's a solid gal. Doin' a hell of a job out there."

We were back on safe ground. Talk of work and achievements came easily to him. We chatted for awhile about the city of Cincinnati and Molly's success at the nursing home.

When the check came, I insisted on paying and he thanked me. I quickly retreated to the safety of Bufford and headed to Bob's house.

???

Sheena Easton announced a late-August concert date at a theme park between Rochester and Buffalo. When I saw the notice in the paper, I raced to Caroline's house. Together, we drove to the mall to buy tickets. The concert would take place just a few days before I left for Cincinnati.

I'd finally see her in person! "I don't care how much it costs," I told Caroline, as we stepped into the ticket office. "I *have* to be in the front row."

"Absolutely," she replied.

The kid at the ticket counter looked bored with my request. "It's general admission because it's an outdoor concert with lawn seating. If you want a front-row seat, you have to get there early and be the first through the door."

I took the tickets and turned to Caroline. "We're getting there two—no, three hours early."

She nodded in agreement.

???

Near the end of July, the gang planned one, last, guys-only drinking bash at Duck Lake. Tim and I headed to Gerard's Grocery to pick up two cases of Moosehead. Pushing Bufford just past the speed limit, we arrived at D.L. before the others.

Within an hour, John pulled up in his family's beat-up Impala. Bob, Roy, John, Peter, Chips, and Bill spilled out of the doors.

All eight of us together.

The beer and profanity flowed in regular proportions. Bob stuck to his soda. I cracked open an ice-cold brew, foam spilling onto my new LIFE'S A BITCH AND THEN YOU DIE tee shirt. Anne had given it to me for my eighteenth birthday.

"To D.L.!" I said, holding my bottle in the air. The other guys pulled close.

John cheered, "the happiest fuckin' place on Earth!" and drained his bottle.

"Chug – chug – chug," we chanted, each downing the beer in our hands, then visiting the ancient Duck Lake refrigerator for another.

Over the afternoon, we toasted the cottage, McQuaid, the Jesuits, our mothers, and Yahtzee. An anxious excitement charged the gathering. We'd soon be heading our separate ways. The loom of college provided an added camaraderie.

Breaking from the rest, Roy and I rowed out onto the lake in my rubber raft. Reaching the midpoint, I swapped manning the oars for a bottle of Moosehead, which Roy had carried for me from shore.

Taking the beer he offered, I laughed to myself, thinking about my initial reaction to him – and the triangle he'd unwittingly created with me and Bob. I was glad I'd traded caution for friendship. *Besides*, I thought, *Bob is with Beth now.*

I took a gulp of the chilly brew. "We still got time to come here for one more party. We can bring the Mercy girls," I offered. I wasn't ready for this to be a final trip.

"You bring the beer, I'll be here." Roy took a long swig from his bottle. "This is a good time, Grey-g," he said.

"D.L. is the best," I said. "We gotta keep it in my family forever."

"We can buy it as a group and have all our reunions here!" he laughed.

The pleasant buzz in my head increased my enthusiasm. "That's a fuckin' awesome idea! We'll tell the other guys when we get back."

"Fuckin' - A!" he shouted.

We clinked bottles to seal the deal. Later, back at the cottage, the others agreed it was a good plan.

Tuesday, July 31, 1984
Last Friday, July 27th, Tim called me at the store around 9:30AM and told me that Roy was killed in a car accident that morning. I couldn't believe it.

The phone had rung at Gerard's Grocery early on Friday.

I worked the counter. Mormon season geared up to its usual frenzy. Two tour busses pulled into the parking lot at the same time, each unloading a horde of thirsty, hungry pilgrims. Paul, Dad, and I opened three registers, but we barely kept up with the traffic.

Paul answered the phone, listened, then said "Greg, it's for you."

"Who is it?" I snapped at him, scooping bottles of caffeine-free juice into a paper sack.

"I think it's Tim."

I pulled away from the counter and grabbed the receiver. It *was* Tim.

"What's goin' on?" I said over the commotion surrounding me.

"Ummm, I have some bad news," his voice cracked.

I had never known Tim's voice to crack.

"What's goin' on?"

"There was a car accident this morning – and Roy's dead."

My whole body froze. It was as though the guy with the ski mask had returned, pointing his ice-cold shotgun at my face. The din of the customers faded into the background.

"*What*?" I gripped the phone receiver tightly, mashing it against my ear so I could hear better. "*What happened*?"

"He was driving to work at the golf course this morning and a car slid into his lane. There was a propane tank in the van and it burned up."

"Where?" My mind reeled, wanting details, trying to get some purchase on the information I was hearing.

Tim's voice was barely audible. "On the hill near his house, coming down to the plaza."

I put my hand on the counter to steady myself, its familiar vinyl grounding the rest of me.

"When?"

"Around five-thirty this morning."

"Oh my gosh. Oh my gosh." *We just went to Duck Lake on Tuesday. I was just with Roy on Tuesday and now he's dead.*

Like one of my grandmother's tragic stories come to life.

"How do you know?"

"One of the Smiths' friends called my mom. She's on her way over there right now."

"Did you call any of the guys yet?"

"No, but Bob knows, he and his family are already over there."

"Oh my gosh."

I looked out at the bustling crowd of customers piling their snacks onto the counter.

"Ummm, I'll call John and Chips, you call Peter and Bill. Let's—" I hesitated. I needed to organize – formulate a game plan – and gain control of the situation.

"Let's meet at the apartment and we'll go over to the Smiths' from there. Tell 'em to meet at—" I looked at the neon beer clock above the back counter. The dial read nine-thirty. "—meet at noon."

"Okay."

"Okay, I just need to confirm with you, before I start callin' people, you said that Roy's dead, right?"

Tim's reply was lifeless. "Yeah, that's right."

"Okay, I'll see you at noon."

I hung up the receiver and stood facing the stickers on the wall above the phone. The words *Ontario County Sheriff* stared at me, the same sticker I'd used when I was robbed.

I should be crying, I thought.

I turned around and looked at a Mormon boy, too young to know that he wasn't supposed to consume caffeine, pulling chocolate bars from the wire rack.

Paul looked up from the register between customers. "What's wrong?" I stared at my brother and his lumpy skull. *I always thought my brother would be the one to die, not my friend. Paul was the death I'd been prepared for.* I sucked in a mouthful of air. "Tim said that Roy died in a car accident this morning."

My brother's face clouded. Dad looked over, turning his back on a man at the counter.

"What?" Dad asked.

I repeated the message.

My father scowled, then looked at Paul. I turned away from them and dialed Big Brick. Mom answered.

I told her what had happened.

"*What-t?*"

I heard her voice break and imagined the tears that were already forming on her cheeks. "Roy is dead. He had a car accident this morning. I'm gonna call the other guys and then we're meeting to go over to the Smiths'. I'll stop by and get my stuff on the way."

"Okay, Honey. Drive safely," she managed.

The line went dead.

Paul and Dad continued to ring up groceries, glancing over at me between orders, as I called John at his summer job. I went through it with him just as Tim had with me.

Roy is dead.

It hit me again like a bucket of icy water.

"Are you sure?" John asked, his voice cracking like Tim's.

"Yeah. I double checked before we hung up." I could feel his shock through the phone line.

We agreed to meet at the Apt. I hung up, repeated the call with Chips, then turned to Paul and Dad. I gave them a quick overview of my game plan as the customers stood patiently in line. "I need to head out."

"No problem," Dad said.

I drove home in a fog, reviewing the conversation with Tim again and again. *Had I heard him right?* It didn't seem real. The drone of Bufford's tires against the hot summer pavement reminded me I wasn't dreaming.

At home, Mom met me at the door. "Oh my baby," she said, hugging me with one hand, rosary beads clutched against her breast with the other. Her eyes were damp as I'd imagined.

I broke away after a minute. "I gotta hurry to meet the guys." I rushed up the staircase.

"Don't race!" my mother screamed after me.

"Don't worry about me," I said.

In the privacy of my room, I continued my planning. What did I need? I pushed my Lifesavers bag aside. I wouldn't be taking pictures or making crime sketches today.

I gathered a stack of photos, from Duck Lake, from school, from different parties we'd been to. Pictures seemed useful, somehow.

The tee shirt I'd worn on Tuesday night lay across a stack of dirty clothes in the corner. My eye caught the words BITCH and DIE. I grabbed it from the pile and spread it across my lap.

LIFE'S A BITCH AND THEN YOU DIE.

The last shirt I'd worn in front of Roy.

Guilty sweat began to moisten my armpits.

Roy is dead and that's the last thing he saw me in.

Shame washed over me in a torrent, stinging my eyes, causing my hands to tremble. All my humiliations – masturbation, magazines, desires – rose to a frenzied pitch inside.

I hadn't welcomed Roy at first because I wanted my after-school rides alone with Bob. *I missed time to know Roy because I like boys. And now he's dead.*

I glanced up at the Sheena Easton poster I'd taped to the ceiling above my bed. I'd placed it there to inspire my desire, but nothing had taken root. I shook my head without speaking.

I grabbed the tee shirt at the collar and yanked. It stretched, but the material refused to rip. I pulled harder, my stomach knotting as tightly as the folds of the material between my fingers. Despite my Herculean efforts, the cloth held. My arm muscles began to jitter.

It was no use.

Wrapping the shirt into a tight ball, I stuffed it deep into the garbage can next to my desk. Scooping up the photos, I ran down the stairs and headed out to Bufford. Behind me, my mother called out another warning to drive safely.

Tuesday, July 31, 1984 (continued)

We had just gone to Duck Lake last Tuesday nite – the whole gang. We had the best time – played Yahtzee, then Roy and I took a short raft ride. I remember a dead fish went under us and when we looked for it later, we couldn't find it. He and John took a piss in the woods, and afterwards he said, "Two or three shakes, John?" I remember the way he said "Grey-g." God, he was so alive. I miss him, and I hardly appreciated him when he was here. I think he knows that now. It's been a hard weekend.

222

I spent Friday with Peter, John, and Tim at the Apt, calling people. We went as a group to the Smith's around 6:10PM – at first it was not bad. Later, I was starting to feel really bad seeing his sister, Alison, and his mom and dad so crushed. When his mom told us they were burying him in his Hawaiian t-shirt and flag shorts and running shoes, I almost sobbed. I wanted to sob freely, but it just wouldn't come.

I slept at Bob's house. I asked him to give me a back rub but first a hug, and we lay there on the cushions for about 5 minutes. It was the best hug of my life. He gave me a long back rub that eased the tension, and then I hugged him for another 5 minutes. It felt so good. I love him so much, and I miss Roy so much.

Saturday I woke and cried a little more. Especially when I read the newspaper article that Roy was alive after the crash and his hands were flailing, and a guy tried to save him. I felt so bad.

I went to work at the store and was busy all day with the Mormons. Then Beth and Sue showed up at Gee's (9:30PM.) We went to Sue's for swimming. Sue said on the way she wished the news wouldn't keep saying 'a man was killed,' because Roy was just a kid, but I sorta don't want to take that away from Roy. He was a man, and a neat one. This has made us all very close, but at what a price. It's aged us, too.

Sunday, instead of going to Church, I went to the cemetery in Macedon and cried a little. I couldn't imagine Roy in a place like that. It was a beautiful day, and nature turned my head. For a little while, anyway.

Monday was the funeral. It was beautiful, but so sad. I felt so bad, to have us sitting there and have Roy be in the casket. I cried some. The priest said Roy felt no pain, he was in shock. All seven of us rode from the church to the cemetery in Bufford, for old times' sake. We were joking a little bit in the car, then we got to the cemetery.

It was the ultimate sorrow. Roy's mom tapped the casket and I wanted to sob. Bob's face was so full of pain and tears were running down his cheeks and I wanted to make it right but I couldn't. We went back to Roy's for food, and all I could think was that we looked so old sitting around eating and talking.

Roy's sister, Alison, showed me some of Roy's Mt. God book. In the notebook, Father O. gave us an assignment to write a personal epitaph. Roy wrote:

He stayed on the offensive to open doors rather than putting up defenses. – Roy Smith

Pretty neat. What a guy. God must love him a lot to call him to Heaven and cause us this sorrow.

Tuesday was a good recovery day. It's been a tough, maturing weekend. I love You, my Lord, and I thank You for such <u>wonderful</u>, loving friends.

I love you, Roy.

RUNAWAY PLAN: Cincinnati/Day Sixty-Three (1984)

I was now completely freed from college.

Euphoria flushed across the surface of my mind – successfully masking the darker thoughts lurking beneath.

Chapter Thirteen: Acorns Dropping (1984 continued)

LIFE TOOK ON an urgency I hadn't known before Roy's death.

Everything was intensified. Every feeling, every thought was now an amplified version of its previous expression.

My burning attraction to boys threatened to overwhelm me.

What if I died?

Would I go to hell because of what I'd done with Adam?

What I wanted to do with Bob?

I hated that everybody else seemed to talk about their attractions without any filtering. The customers at Gee's, the guys at school, Beth, Merk. Even the Opes had faded pictures of their husbands or wives on their dressers.

The normalcy was beyond my grasp. I couldn't even seem to admit my desire to myself. I hinted at my longings in my journal writings, but the next entry always reversed the suggestion.

Would I ever be attracted to girls? Sheena looked gorgeous, staring down at me from the ceiling, but the knowledge never made it below my neck. In my bed alone, my heart – and parts lower – wanted to be with Bob. The *Human Sexuality* promise I'd clung to for so many years seemed empty and inadequate.

In my mind, I pulled my life apart and reconnected it, but the fix – the solution that would make it work in a way that would please everybody – eluded my best Jupiter-logic.

I couldn't solve the mystery of my sexuality.

I could still be a priest, I recalled my boyhood desire. Celibacy could solve my struggle permanently, but I wasn't sure I liked that solution. A vow of chastity meant no sex, *ever.* I still couldn't make it a single day without my nighttime habit.

Please God, I prayed in my bedroom, thinking of Roy in the burning van. *Help me find Your way for me in this world.*

The next evening was cooler as August began to wind down. I had to leave for Cincinnati in one week.

After dinner, I walked across the street. Caroline and I sat alone at the top of their backyard hill, talking about what had happened to Roy and the upcoming Sheena concert.

I could see the creek knotting through the woods below. The island where we'd made up a game about being stranded at sea. The weathered shed we'd pretended belonged to a hermit with a secret past.

Nostalgia washed over me everywhere I looked. I would miss all of this. I would miss her. Maybe that's all love was — feeling loss when someone wasn't there. An idea fluttered through my brain. I pushed it down, but it surfaced again with more determination.

I loved Caroline. And trusted her.

Why couldn't I be normal?

I diverted my thoughts with a question. "Are you gonna be lonely, without having me across the street?"

She laughed. "I'll survive. But you better write to me a lot."

I paused, looking toward the sun's last warm rays on the barn below us. "You know, I was sorta thinkin', you and I are pretty compatible."

She nodded.

I continued, fumbling for words. "What would you think about us getting married?"

She didn't laugh, but her face twisted with surprise. "Are you crazy? You're heading off to Cincy in a week!"

"I know that. It doesn't have to be right away, but I was just thinking about how well we get along and what the future could be like."

Silence fell between us, broken only by a cricket, which had begun to wail in the nearby field.

"I guess—" she trailed off. "I guess I'm flattered."

I pressed for a more definite response as need gripped me, craving normalcy, wanting to remove the burden that had weighed on me for five years. *Being married would solve so many of my problems.* "That doesn't answer my question."

She drew her feet up close under her summer dress, hugging her legs to her chest. "Greg, for Heaven's sake, I'm fifteen years old!" she answered. "I mean I love you, don't take this the wrong way. I think of you as a best friend, or as the brother I never had. But I think the answer to your question is that I'm only fifteen."

She spoke carefully, concern evident in her tone. "I haven't even dated a boy yet. Maybe we could think about this again later. When I'm older. Please don't think this means I don't care about you!"

I stared at my lap. "You're right. I'm sorry, it's just been really tough the last couple of weeks."

My eyes filled with tears. I blinked hard, willing them away. She was one of the people I trusted most, but I could not let her in on my private shame.

She didn't move any closer. My heart swelled with gratitude for her companionship as we sat on the lawn in comfortable silence, dusk fading into night.

???

I had only one Sunday left in Pal-Mac. Instead of going to Mass, I found myself driving around in Bufford. I visited Gram's grave, then Saint Michael's. I sat in the parking lot of my grammar school and talked to God, about His will, about my purpose.

After what happened to Roy, the banality of *Stand – Sit – Kneel* had lost its familiar comfort.

The next day, I called the guys and girls with plans for one last gathering before I headed west. Everyone accepted.

Duck Lake seemed the appropriate location, where we'd always partied, where we'd last been with Roy. I assembled small photo albums as a goodbye gift for my friends. They were filled with pictures of Roy.

The day of the party, John drove out to Big Brick so we could ride together on this last excursion to D.L.

"Hey, John," I said as he stepped out of his car.

Greeting any of the guys felt charged now.

"Hey." We paused, then hugged quickly.

"Let's get this show on the road!" I said as we started pulling party gear from the back of his beat-up Impala and loading it into Bufford's trunk.

"We going by Gee's?" he asked as he balanced the large brown cooler, the one I'd asked him to bring. "I figured we could load up with ice and Moose there."

"That's my plan."

"Very good!"

We finished packing the car, then said a quick goodbye to Mom. She handed me a foil package. A familiar scent of chocolate hit my nose. "I thought you boys could use some fudge," she said.

"Thanks," I smiled and hugged her.

"Be careful!" she yelled down the sidewalk as John and I walked toward the car.

"Yessss, Mother." I dragged out the phrase – to make it clear I was too old for mothering.

We arrived at my parents' cottage a couple of hours before the others. John and I set up the cooler and snacks, then I cracked open two Michelobs, our alternate beer choice. "No Moosehead yet," I said, handing one of the bottles to him.

"Agreed."

John took a deep swig of the beer, then sat at the table looking out over the tranquil lake. "It's still seems so hard to believe. We were just here with him two weeks ago."

"I keep forgetting he's gone," I said, sitting down. "I mean, I know he's gone, but I keep thinking of stuff that I want to tell him and I remember I can't."

We tilted our bottles again.

I continued. "I was right out there with him in the raft. We were talking about pooling resources to buy D.L."

John smiled. "Did I ever tell you about the day Roy was driving me home from golfing and he almost hit a squirrel?"

I shook my head.

"We were just messing around, he saw a squirrel near the curb and yells "five points!" and swerves. He was just joking around, he swerved right back, I mean, he wasn't really gonna hit the squirrel or anything. But two seconds later there are flashing lights behind us!"

It was my turn to smile.

"Did he get a ticket?"

"Nahhh, the cop just wanted to see his license and asked him what was goin' on. Roy told him he was tryin' to miss a squirrel in the road. We didn't mention that he was going for it in the first place!"

John and I laughed. Telling stories about Roy helped vent some of the maudlin feeling that had taken root inside my gut over the past couple of weeks.

We traded stories all afternoon, reliving other memories of Duck Lake, McQuaid classes, Headquarters visits.

Bob's car finally pulled into the cottage's small yard. Beth and Bob sat in front. Bob's sister and Roy's sister squished out of the backseat.

I hugged them each, lingering for a moment with Bob, then pulling quickly away. "Well, we've got a party to plan!" I broke the uncomfortable silence.

Everyone took a task: light the grill, shape hamburger patties, prep macaroni salad. Sue soon arrived with a car full of Mercy girls. Peter and Tim showed up with Bill and Chips. Nobody wanted to miss the final party.

"Moosehead tribute to Roy at eight o'clock!" I announced to the crowd, touching the twenty-four bottles of Moosehead snuggled in the ice chest.

The sun hung low over the water when we finished eating. Bob and Beth left for a walk along the channel while Sue and I gathered plates.

I checked the clock and pulled open the brown cooler. "Fifteen minutes 'til the tribute to Roy!"

At eight sharp I made sure everybody had a beer in their hand, even the younger girls. "Hey, Bob and Beth aren't here," John pointed out.

"Bob doesn't drink," I said. "I said we were doing this at eight. I'm thinkin' he didn't want to be here."

We huddled together in the cottage's living room as the sun dipped toward the horizon across the lake. "Here's to Roy," we said, lifting our bottles toward the ceiling. Everybody drank. Quiet settled over the cabin.

A fish broke across the surface of the lake, sending ripples in every direction. I watched the rings expand across the water, moving away and disappearing.

Like Roy had done.

My eyes moistened as I broke the silence. "I have a going-away present for everybody." Reaching into my book bag, I distributed the miniature photo albums I'd prepared. The gang broke into groups, looking at the pictures, drinking their Moosehead. Someone put the Animal House soundtrack on the stereo and increased the volume. Sue and the other girls danced.

Bob and Beth returned about ten minutes later. As soon as they came through the door, I rushed over. "You missed the tribute. Did you not wanna do it?" I asked.

Bob looked at me, his face twisting with an unreadable emotion. He spun around and went back outside.

My stomach tightened as I looked at Beth. She waved me by her. "It's okay, go get him," she said. I stepped outside. Bob leaned against Bufford. His mouth quivered.

I approached. "Bob, I'm so sorry! I thought since you didn't drink beer, you were skipping it."

He looked at the ground, wiping at his eyes with his right hand. "I was gonna have one for Roy."

We stood in unbearable silence.

This is my fault, I thought. I wanted to make it right. I wanted to hug him – to *kiss* him – and whisper that I was sorry. My arms remained locked at my sides. The pain of resisting made my head feel swollen and heavy. My stomach wrenched tight.

John interrupted us. Three Moosehead bottles dangled between his fingers. "Let's have our own tribute," he said. With a visible relief, Bob and I accepted the beer from him.

We popped the caps and lifted the bottles as tension drained out of me in a wave. John had somehow fixed the moment.

"For Roy," I said for the second time that day.

As we quietly guzzled the beer, I caught the sound of acorns dropping in the woods beyond the road. I listened to the tiny impacts, wondering at the simplicity.

Acorns needed to fall, so they fell.

Tears welled in my eyes again. I successfully contained every single one.

John, Bob, and I traded more stories of Roy under the darkening trees. We huddled, talking and laughing, until we could no longer see the pale reflection of sky on the surface of the lake. Finally, we returned to the cottage, where the rest of the group danced madly to ear-splitting decibels of Animal House's *Shout*.

RUNAWAY PLAN: Cincinnati/Day Sixty-Three continued (1984)

The rush of having no commitments, not college, not even Sunday Mass, carried me through the whole day. In the evening, Molly donned her bone-white nursing uniform and headed to work.

"See ya later, Caboose," she joked. I followed her as far as the stairwell window and watched her walk safely to the car.

Coming back into the apartment, the reality of the last two days struck me. After almost ten years, I was no longer a Catholic schoolboy.

I don't belong anywhere.

I was freed from all responsibility – I wasn't even paying Molly rent – but the intoxication of the freedom oozed away, leaving the dull ache of a mystery unsolved.

What am I gonna do?

My same struggle surfaced, the same gurgitation in my belly.

Was I supposed to be a priest?

Would I ever want to marry a woman?

Would anything ever fill the gnawing emptiness in my heart?

I needed something to munch on.

I went into the kitchen and opened the refrigerator. A jug of milk and a bottle of ketchup stood alone on the shelves. A solitary orange lay in the corner of the crisper.

My stomach grumbled in response. I scrounged through the cupboards.

They were empty.

Panic gripped me. I had no job, no purpose – and I had no food.

Chapter Fourteen: Escape (1984 continued)

THE DAY BEFORE the concert, I went to the mall and had six tee shirts made, each bearing a single letter, S-H-E-E-N-A. Sue, Beth, Bob, Kathy, Caroline and I planned to wear them.

I worked to maintain my enthusiasm for the show, despite everything that had happened. My dream of meeting Sheena was a pleasant distraction from the sadness surrounding Roy.

The day of the concert, everyone piled in Bufford. I cranked the song *Telefone* as we drove to the theme park, four hours before the concert start time.

Everyone else headed for the rides, but Caroline and I went directly to the concert shell. Three people already stood in line. We joined as the fourth and fifth. Sitting on the cooler I'd brought, we endured the lengthy wait, chatting with the other kids in line. When the doors opened an hour later, we raced in and threw a blanket down center front.

"Is this good?" I asked Caroline, scanning the surroundings as the rest of the front-row spots filled in. A wire fence and thirty feet beyond separated the audience from the raised stage. I wanted to be closer, but this would have to do.

"It's fine," she replied. "Come on, let's buy some programs."

"You go. I'll stay here and guard the blanket." I handed her forty dollars in cash. "Get me one of everything I don't have," I said.

Caroline returned a short time later with a Sheena program, Sheena head shot, and Sheena shoelaces. The rest of the gang eventually showed up. Standing together, our six shirts spelled out Sheena's first name in bright letters. I fidgeted on the blanket, waiting for the concert to begin. Beth looked over my purchases. "Sheena *shoelaces*?" she groaned.

I laughed. "I'm a fan, alright already?"

We didn't wait long. In less than thirty minutes, musicians walked onstage and began to tune their instruments. A driving beat started up. I recognized the beginning of the song, *Modern Girl*, the same instant Sheena walked onto the stage!

The six of us jumped up and cheered. Sheena must have noticed our shirts, for she pointed directly at us and did a half-bow, half-laugh.

I felt my cheeks warm with embarrassment – and grand satisfaction.

She wore white summer shorts and a frilly yellow blouse. Her hair was fluffed into a huge tangle of curls, which surrounded her face. She was as gorgeous in person as on the album covers.

My favorite music began to fill the evening air. I sang along, smiling at Caroline and the rest of the girls. Sue turned to me. "You know, I can hear you anytime – tonight, I'd like to hear her!" I laughed and tried to restrain my excitement.

After the first couple of songs, Sheena stopped singing to talk to the audience. Caroline leaned over and whispered in my ear. "She has an engagement ring on." I spotted the ring on Sheena's finger and knew what Caroline was referring to.

Just a few nights earlier, we'd watched Sheena on *The Tonight Show*. Joan Rivers, the guest host, had heckled Sheena for telling the audience about her engagement, but having no ring to display. 'Sheena, get a ring!' Joan had commanded.

I thought about it. Here was something I could bring up. Something I could actually talk to Sheena about. Something other people might not think of.

I had to do it.

A moment later, Sheena paused during her banter with the audience. I took a deep breath and yelled "You got a ring!"

Sheena looked my way. "What?" She cupped her ear.

I turned up the volume. "YOU GOT A RING!"

She laughed, nodded, and displayed her hand. "Yeah, Joan Rivers talked him into it."

My heart beat twice as fast as normal. I had actually talked to Sheena Easton! Caroline patted me on the back. "Nice job," she whispered.

My pulse barely slowed during the rest of the concert. Sheena changed clothes twice, finally wearing a glittery short-short dress. As the end of the concert approached, the six of us stood as a group and surged forward, pressing against the fence that separated the audience from the stage. My idol stood close.

My whole body tensed, as if the moment I'd been expecting since puberty might suddenly blossom. My "Sophia Loren" moment.

Up close, Sheena was shorter in real life than I'd expected. But still as stunningly feminine as the album covers, as the poster over my bed. Inside my chest, my heart pounded. I waited for something – anything – to stir inside of me down lower.

Nothing happened. No fantastic surge of heterosexuality coursed through my body. No full adolescent responsiveness.

Dancing wildly with the rest of the crowd as the finale song, *Morning Train,* pounded, for a brief moment, I offered up all the things that troubled me, releasing them into the warm night air.

My unfulfilled longings for Bob.

Roy's death.

Abomination.

Hell.

The show ended, Sheena said goodbye, and my life returned.

???

Over the years, I had seen Molly, Kathy, Mike, and Anne each pack their cars and make that last trip down the winding driveway of Big Brick. Now it was my turn.

I'd spent Friday night at the Apt, saying my goodbyes to Anne and Kathy. Anne and I each downed a Sunkist screwdriver, for old time's sake. "You guys will come visit Cincinnati, won't you?" I asked through a pleasant vodka buzz.

"I guess we'll manage it," Anne joked, punching my arm. "Somebody's got to look out for you, little brother."

On Saturday and Sunday I'd jammed my belongings into every available inch of Bufford. The backseat wasn't visible beneath my Stephen King collection, my Three Investigators books, my typewriter, clothes, letters, my Lifesavers bag. The trunk held a similar collection. Everything I'd amassed over eighteen years.

Nestled in the center of the front bench seat were the things I had a more immediate need for: Sheena cassettes, the road atlas, my college acceptance packet. I left the rider's seat available for Molly, who flew home to make the drive back to Cincinnati with me.

My porn collection was safe. I'd merged the men and women magazines and packed them securely in the corner of HQ under the work shelf. As added protection, I'd installed a padlock on the ceiling hatch. Nobody would be viewing the contents of Headquarters without my presence.

Standing on Big Brick's stoop, I stretched my Sheena tee shirt material with my fist, trying to make it baggier around the stomach area. Mom's eyes were teary, although her face was dry. She pulled me close. "Be careful, Honey. Drive safely."

"I *will*, Mother!"

I tried my best to sound annoyed, although a mixture of emotions rolled around my gut, a casserole of nostalgia, guilt, excitement, and relief.

Dad spoke next. "Take care, Caboose. Show those birds up ·at Xavier how it's done."

I hugged him for the first time since I was little boy, an awkward, chubby embrace. It seemed the right thing to do, considering our Perkins talk just a few weeks earlier.

"I'll try," I said, quickly pulling away.

Our dog, Pete, struggled to rise from his napping spot on the porch. He'd become arthritic in his older years – we hadn't been out to the field together in a long time.

"See ya, Boy," I said, rubbing his soft fur and staring into his watery eyes. Predictably, he smothered my face in kisses.

One of the Opes, a white-haired woman named Marie who now occupied Gram's bedroom, pulled her window curtain aside and peered out at the commotion. I waved. She waved back.

Paul accompanied me down the sidewalk, limping slightly as he went. It had started sometime after the last surgery – his right leg dragged just a hair behind the left – and became more pronounced when he was tired. I ignored his gait as he kept pace with me.

"Well, I guess this is it," I said, reaching Bufford. I opened the driver's door and stood there. Molly hopped into the rider's seat.

"Do they have Perkins in Cincinnati?" Paul joked.

"I'm sure they do," I laughed.

"I'll be there."

He stepped forward unexpectedly and grasped me around the middle. We'd never hugged before. I patted his back and we broke apart, neither of us speaking. I got into the car and waved to all of them through Bufford's windshield. The casserole churned.

"Let's get the hell out of here," Molly said. "I hate these drawn-out goodbye scenes."

I began to giggle, venting some of the angst that had gathered inside. It was a good distraction from the tension of the last weeks.

As I eased the car back, mentally preparing to make my own last trip down the driveway, Mom rushed down the sidewalk, waving frantically. I pressed the brake and rolled down my window.

"Don't race!" she yelled.

I rolled my eyes and smiled. "Yes, Mom!"

Pushing firmly on the accelerator, we headed out.

We made a final trip to Gerard's Grocery to fill Bufford's gas tank and stock up on trip snacks. The windows were dark. Paul wouldn't open the doors for another thirty minutes.

Molly picked out a few Hershey bars and a bag of pork rinds. "Grab some pretzel rods and plain M&Ms," I requested over the buzz of the gas pump monitor.

Adding some bottles of 7-UP to our collection, I tallied the bill and put the slip into the cash register. My last free purchase.

Locking the door behind us, I piled back into the car next to my sister and drove around the perimeter of the building. Pulling onto the highway, the tailpipe scrapped against the ground; Bufford was riding low from the load.

The long drive along Interstate 90 reminded me of the trip to Myrtle Beach just four months before. *When everything was different.* I thought about the extra goodbye I'd shared with Bob just two days ago.

After Saturday dinner, I'd driven to his house. Saying goodbye with the group at Duck Lake hadn't been enough for the two of us. We hung out in his room, listening to his albums, talking about Roy. I longed for one last backrub, but in the charged atmosphere, I felt awkward and exposed.

"So are you and Beth gonna keep dating in college?" I asked. Beth planned to leave for Cornell University soon. Bob would stay in town, starting at Saint John Fisher, a local Catholic college, in a week.

He looked at his lap. "We've been talkin' about it. Pretty much all the time. Ultimately, I don't think so."

He raised his head. His eyes glistened.

My own eyes moistened, but I remained riveted to the chair next to his built-in desk. "I'm sorry, man," I said quietly. My heart thumped so loudly in my ears I feared he would hear it.

Later, after more talk and more Billy Joel, dusk trickled through the maple and pine trees that lined his street. We drifted outside and stood by my car.

"I guess this is it," I said.

"Yeah, I guess so."

"I'll be home at Thanksgiving. We'll have a reunion at D.L. With *everybody*."

"You better write, man. I'm gonna be the only one left in this town," he said.

"You can *count* on it."

We pulled each other close for a full minute, then I stepped into Bufford and drove away.

My thoughts returned to Interstate 90. Driving to college. I shifted my head toward the driver's window, so Molly couldn't see the emotions that threatened to expose me. I silently prayed that my escape to Cincinnati – being away from the turmoil and tension of home – would set everything in my life right.

.

RUNAWAY PLAN: Cincinnati/Day Sixty-Three continued (1984)

I grabbed Bufford's keys from the edge of the kitchen counter. Scooping change from my bedroom coin dish into my jeans pocket, I headed down the stairs, two at a time.

I needed to eat.

In the car, I rushed out of the Park At Your Own Risk lot. Bufford's tires spat gravel in my wake.

Reaching the grocery store, I headed for the snack aisle. Pulling coins out of my pocket, I counted out five dollars in quarters. I miss Gerard's Grocery, I thought, grabbing at a dollar bag of pretzel rods. With limited funds, I could only afford to add a medium-sized bag of M&Ms and a one-liter bottle of 7-UP. It would be enough.

Rushing through the express lane, I hopped into the front seat of my car and yanked at the candy bag. A jagged slit tore down the side as pieces of chocolate flew onto the floor and disappeared down the crack of the seat.

"Shit!" I swore, trying to contain the rest.

I poured the remaining M&Ms into my car's drink tray and opened the pretzel bag more carefully. Positioning them on the seat next to me, I began to chew, watching the people come and go.

A man and woman rode up on bicycles. They pulled their bikes together, locking them to a pole in front of the store. Two teenage girls giggled as they walked through a group of parking-lot pigeons. An older couple loaded brown grocery bags into the back seat of a station wagon like Dad's. I could faintly hear them arguing.

Everybody was in pairs. Everybody seemed to know who they were. And how to belong. Everybody except me.

I turned the key in Bufford's ignition and tore out of the brightly lit lot. Pigeons scattered in my wake.

Continuing to cram pretzel rods into my mouth, I headed down the one-way street, away from our Park at Your Own Risk apartment.

I had to move. I had to think.

I headed toward the river.

Sheena's Best Kept Secret cassette was still in the stereo. I cranked up the volume and rolled down both front windows.

Streetlights flashed like lightning into the car's interior as I raced through the city. I pulled onto Route 50, the five-lane highway that hugged the river's bank for miles. I pushed harder on Bufford's accelerator.

Thoughts rushed at me as quickly as the night air that whipped past my head. The speedometer jumped as I worked to outrun them.

Route 50 goes all the way to Ocean City. I could go there.

You don't have enough money for gas, the Jupiter part of my mind whispered back.

The drop-off to the river's edge increased as I left city limits. Sheena's driving beat cut through me. I could feel the bass pounding in my chest, in my belly. I was glad there were hardly any other cars on the road.

I thought about the conversation with my dad, telling him I wanted to quit college. It conjured the image of him sitting at Big Brick's kitchen table years before, a glass of scotch in his hand, deciding that I, The Caboose, would be the only one of his children to attend Catholic school.

My stomach groaned.

Other images emerged from the rush around me. The shotgun pointed at my chest during the store robbery. My nightly habit in my Big Brick bedroom. Dead flies trapped in the ceiling fixture.

Shame and fear flushed fresh and bitter into my throat.

Thoughts of Roy surfaced. The raft floating on Duck Lake. Hands flailing in the burning van. Hot tears struggled to flow from the corners of my eyes. I fought them, turning up the radio another *notch. I glanced at the mucky water of the Ohio River, but its dark surface reflected only secrets.*

Nothing worked. Not quitting college. Not eating my favorite snacks. Not driving eighty miles an hour.

I just couldn't escape.

Why couldn't I be like everybody else?

From beneath the churning M&M/pretzel/7-UP whirlpool in my stomach, the answer to my life's mystery struggled to belch forth.

My hands shook as I shoveled snacks into my mouth. Bufford skittered on the pavement in response as Sheena's voice screamed Let Sleeping Dogs Lie *from the stereo.*

Choices hovered like an all-you-can-eat buffet in my mind.

Father O'Malley had taught me to seek things out. He wanted me to question, to be bold. To value truth. To think.

I could learn his lesson or I could continue to follow the river, living in the shadows of everyone else's expectations – everyone else's view of whom I should be.

The Church, my family, my teachers, my friends – my detective hero, Jupiter – had both helped and hindered *me in my quest to know myself. Even God had seemed both to comfort and condemn me in my struggle. I'd spent years trying to solve it, trying to fix it, trying to* offer it up. *Years waiting for lightning to strike me dead.*

I was tired. It was time for me to ease up on the gas and put a key piece of the puzzle into place.

The answer erupted to the surface.

I'm not attracted to girls because I'm gay.

I stopped chewing. I had studied it, prayed about it, fantasized with it, but never actually believed *it.*

I am gay.

Another thought jumped in. That's it?

I had struggled for almost five years. I wanted a scientific and complex resolution, grand and dramatic. Something Jupiter would be proud of.

My cheeks worked to flush with embarrassment at my stupidity. I resisted, as another stronger feeling washed through me.

Relief.

Somehow, despite the simplicity of my revelation, admitting *it to myself – without an excuse, or a penitent prayer, or another mouthful of M&Ms – felt better than any food I'd ever eaten.*

I slowed Bufford at the next cross street and made a wide U-turn away from the river's edge. I considered pulling off to the side of the highway and recording a page for my journal, to capture the moment. I hesitated.

Writing it, or even speaking it, was another level altogether. Just having the realization – just being honest with myself – would do for now.

"Thanks, Jesus," I whispered into the darkened sky and headed back toward the lights of the city.

Chapter Fifteen: My Future Character (1984 continued)

THE NEXT MORNING, I scooped another handful of change from the dish in my room and headed to Wendy's for breakfast.

The relief I'd embraced the night before persisted, but it still hadn't provided me with a purpose. A first next step seemed clear: I had to earn some money.

As I chewed my fried-egg sandwich, I noticed Wendy's had a "Now Hiring" sign taped to the front window. Making a quick decision, I went to the counter and asked for an application. I filled it out while I finished my meal and returned it to the girl at the register.

A manager called me the next day and, after a hasty interview, I picked up my first job since Gerard's Grocery. Being closer to my favorite fast food was a calculated bonus.

It would do until I figured out what came next.

???

The soft glide of autumn brought its usual blend of wistful nostalgia as plants drooped and leaves crumpled onto the pavement. I craved to live in memories. From the apartment building's rooftop, I sought them out in my friends' letters and my own journals.

I continued my pre-college routine: music in my walkman and letters on the roof. It was still summertime warm during the day, but the air temperature plummeted at night.

Most evenings I worked at Wendy's. My paycheck didn't supply as much as the second-drawer down, but it kept Bufford full of gas and left enough money for Sheena's new LP, *A Private Heaven*.

One Tuesday dawned chilly enough to wear a sweatshirt. I yanked on my black and gold McQuaid pullover while Tina Turner's new single, *What's Love Got To Do With It*, blared from the TV. VH1 made a big fuss about the song. I wondered when they'd play Sheena's latest video, *Strut*.

There were no letters in the mailbox, so I packed all my journals into my book bag and headed for the roof. Once there, I emptied the bag. My notes over the years had filled a number of notebooks. In methodical order, I turned slowly through the chronicles of my life.

Gram's death. Longing to be a priest. Paul's surgeries. The bathtub. Adam. Building Headquarters. Saint Mike's graduation. Going to McQuaid. Robberies at Gerard's Grocery. Prayers for normalcy. Backrubs with Bob. Roy's death.

I lay there, awash in nostalgia, needing the certainty I'd felt as a child. "Jesus, You've been a big part of my life," I spoke out loud. "Please, help me find my way now."

Flipping through the pages, an entry from the spring of '81 captured my attention. Back when I was fifteen.

Sunday, May 10, 1981
Today has been so happy. Having most of us home, and the cool/warm springy rain, and the fragrant lilacs. I love the spring. I love my family. Thank You, God, for all You have given us on this beautiful Earth. Oh, how I love the rain, and the wind in the night. It's so adventurous, mysterious, beckoning. I just want to walk in it and hear its patter on the lawn, through the trees, in the gutter.

Homesickness shot through me, more palpable than the effects of any amount of vodka or sugary treat. I missed HQ. Duck Lake. Bob.

When I was little, my grandmother had told her mysterious and tragic tales. I'd longed to find my own adventure like the people in her stories. Somehow, eight years after her death, I now realized that I didn't have to run away to uncover adventure – adventure was available to me anywhere I stood. It didn't require a grand quest, it only demanded my willingness to be honest with myself. *That* was the key to unlocking my adventure. Like Father O. had taught me, I just had to *think*. And that could happen right in the field behind the barn.

I wanna go home.

The feeling was powerful, cutting through my uncertainty of purpose.

I'd have to get a real job and my own apartment. I didn't want to depend on my parents anymore – no more working at Gerard's Grocery, no more listening to Dad ranting through the household – but I knew that Western New York was the familiar surroundings I needed to sort out the mystery of who I would become.

The thought carried the certainty of a flipped switch. There was suddenly no question that I would do anything else.

My prayer stood answered.

I rushed down from the rooftop to call everyone – Mom, Bob, Caroline, Roy's family – everybody I could think of. Their reactions overlapped: surprise at the abruptness, curiosity at my next steps, excitement at seeing me again.

???

When the first hint of frost coated the Cincinnati landscape, I again packed my bedroom of belongings into Bufford.

I said goodbye to the sagging couch, returning it curbside to entice its next owner. Danny helped me carry it out. I said my goodbyes to him as well, looking into his bright blue eyes, wanting to flip his blond bangs aside and pull him close, feeling his arms hug me tight.

Instead, I shook his hand and wished him well.

The next morning Molly and I stood in the parking lot, giggling.

"Don't forget to park at your own risk and run like hell for the door," I told her.

"Put your shoulder to the wheel," she responded.

We laughed. I stepped into my car and waved goodbye.

Bufford rode lower to the ground than when I'd arrived. I'd picked up school textbooks and a new typing desk during my Cincinnati months.

I pulled along Molly's street and stopped at the mailbox on the corner.

The car door scraped against the cement curb as I stepped out, holding an envelope. It was addressed to my brother, Mike, in Virginia.

The day before, I'd stopped at the bank to close out my checking account. Many of the checks still hung unused in the small booklet, a testament to the short duration of my college stay.

The teller, a girl about my age, helped me as I closed the account by endorsing a final check. I meticulously printed $70.90 in the small box – all the money I had in the world. As she searched beneath the back counter for the correct forms, I stood in the white marble lobby and watched the other customers.

Similar to the people in the grocery store parking lot, they seemed busy with purpose, like they had a place to belong, a destination waiting for them.

When would I belong, the way everybody else appeared to ·belong?

My decision was made, my revelation was known, but thoughts about my future still managed to tug at my stomach, threatening to tighten their grip if given enough incentive.

Was I doing the right thing, dropping out of college?

Would Father O'Malley be upset that I've thrown away this chance at higher education or would he applaud the choice as an opportunity to think for myself?

And more importantly, *would I ever figure out what being gay meant for me?*

A memory surfaced, interrupting my thoughts. It was solid, real, and actionable. On impulse, I spoke to the teller, who had returned with a paper for me to sign.

"Can you include a money order for twenty dollars?"

"Sure," she said. "There's a fee of one dollar, though."

"That's fine." I smiled, liking my idea more and more.

The teller filled out a couple of forms and produced my money order. She caught my grin and returned it.

"You heading out of town?" she asked, her tone dipping playfully.

I knew she was flirting. Beth had taught me the signals. Warmth rose in my cheeks. The familiar tightening began in my belly.

I mulled over her question. She was doing what was right for her. It just wasn't right for *me*.

I'd been discovering differences my whole life. Being *The Caboose*, the little brother who wanted to escape. Being the only sibling who went to Catholic school. Being the boy who sought mystery around every corner.

I began to recognize that being gay *was just one more difference*. It was all a part of *being me*. And – for one wonderful moment – I considered that just being me *might be okay*.

The knowledge diffused some of the tension that tried to build inside my tortured gut. "Yeah, out of town," I finally answered.

"That's too bad," she continued the playful tone. "Going anywhere exciting?"

This time I didn't hesitate. "Home. To find myself. Or something like that."

"Oh," she said.

At the mailbox, I drew the twenty-dollar money order from my wallet and wrote *Mike Gerard* in the correct place. On the memo line, I penned *for secret-room-in-the-barn bet, 1974*, then stuffed and sealed the envelope. On the back, I wrote a quick note. *You earned this fair and square. Love, Greg.*

It was only twenty bucks. I'd taken twice that much from the two-fried-eggs sack on the slightest whim. The difference here was that I'd *chosen* to do this, with my *own* money.

The Church hadn't dictated, Dad hadn't yelled, *Human Sexuality* hadn't predicted, Jupiter hadn't modeled.

I was defining my future character.

That rated more than a whole drawer full of money.

I grabbed the handle of the mail slot, deposited the letter, and let the door flip shut. From within, I heard the satisfying sound of the envelope sliding into the guts of the box.

"See ya, Cincinnati," I said out loud and stepped back to the curb, where Bufford was waiting.

Epilogue

Summer 1997

I BACKED MY Civic hatchback up to the barn and slid open the huge door. It creaked along its rail – even more than in my youth.

After twenty years, my family's history still choked the floor: boxes stuffed with curled photos, record albums, lidless Tupperware containers. I pushed past the first few rows, making my way to the piles underneath Headquarters. That's where the more important items, like Gerard's Grocery tax receipts, were stored. That's where I found what I'd come for.

Gram's sewing table.

It had sat in the Old People's living room for a number of years, but after Mom retired – and dismantled the whole Ope setup – the table had made its way out to the barn. I wanted it now for the foyer in my newly purchased Victorian home in Rochester, where my partner and I would make a life together.

I carried my treasure out into the sunlight and brushed the dust from the top, feeling the tickle of a sneeze in the back of my nose. A hint of coconut floated up as I took a moment to poke through the drawers, rediscovering my grandmother. Her button collection. Her address book.

She'd cut small advertisements from the local newspaper and stashed them in the bottom drawer, the same one that had housed the Reese's peanut butter cups so many years before. I laughed aloud, reliving the memory of my runaway plan.

I pulled out a number of clippings and read through a few:

DRESSMAKING: To look your best, your clothes must fit correctly. Call Macedon 6-2329 anytime for reasonable custom dressmaking and alterations.

APPLIANCE REPAIR. All electrical appliances repaired. Toasters, mixers, vacuum cleaners, electric knives, etc. Palmyra 7-6288.

AL'S DELIVERY SERVICE: Appliance and furniture moving. Light hauling, odd jobs. Palmyra 7-5387.

All typical of services my grandmother might use, clipped and stored for easy reference. Relics from a pre-Internet era. I paused for a moment, savoring the bittersweet feel of my youth.

I stuffed the pile of newspaper scraps back into the drawer when one, different from the rest, caught my eye:

STATE NEWS: Fugitive priest wanted for destruction of draft cards shows up at Cornell anti-war rally then disappears again.

The paper was yellowed and faded, but the memory of Gram's stories bloomed fresh and sharp in my mind. I wondered what had motivated her to clip this short note. Had she known the priest? Did she support his cause? Or did she simply place it in the drawer as a reminder, a bit of intrigue to share with me the next time I stopped by for maple walnut ice cream?

A priest working outside of what was *expected* of him — to do what he believed was *right*. In a way, it was similar to my own path, I thought. I still attended church every week, I still talked to God every day — but I also recognized that I didn't fit every person's idea of what a faithful Christian *should be*. And, with the blessing of perspective and grace, how *okay* I was with that.

I tucked the fugitive-priest story back into the sewing table. Its presence was another mystery to add to the fabric of my life, my never-ending quest to seek intrigue. To keep exploring who I was — without trying to escape the truths I uncovered. And most importantly, to think.

Good night shirt.

Reading Group Discussion Guide

1. The author begins the story by introducing a "runaway plan." What things does Greg seek to escape?

2. What does living "in Jupiter's shadow" mean to you? What ways, besides denying their own sexuality, can people live in Jupiter's shadow?

3. What are some of the barriers to Greg's self-awareness of his homosexuality?

4. Greg responds to many different influences telling him who he "should be." Which have the greatest impact on his life, and why?

5. Pop-culture experiences often provide common ground that a memoir author can share with readers. What pop culture is important to Greg? Do the pop-culture references in this story evoke memories for you?

6. The author obviously loves mystery. How has this influenced his writing/storytelling style?

7. Memoir authors have a challenge to avoid overwhelming the reader with characters. In this story, which characters do you find the most compelling? Think about all the people you've known in your life. Which characters would you include in your own memoir?

8. Stomach tension dominates Greg's young life. Locate a scene in the story where the author describes abdominal upset. What emotions do you perceive lurk unexpressed? Do you think Greg is aware of these feelings?

9. The author specifically chose the use of three question marks as scene separators instead of the more traditional asterisks. In the story, he included a clue to the reason for this selection – did you catch it?

10. How does Greg's relationship to his dad evolve during the story? To God? To himself?

11. Death is a universally profound experience. What affect does Roy's death have on Greg's struggle?

12. The author has identified "self-awareness" as a central theme of this story. What additional sub-themes did you identify in your own reading?

A Few Notes from the Author

There are many ways to tell a story. I've had a lot of friends read this one and bring up discussion points. I'll review some of the more common ones here.

TITLE: First, I named this story *In Jupiter's Shadow* for both a literal and a literary reason.

The literal reason: As a kid, I spent a lot of time retreating into the world of mystery and investigation. Jupiter Jones from The Three Investigators was my hero. He was fat and smart; he always beat the crooks. I worked hard to live in his "shadow."

The literary reason: I believe that more-than-their-share of faithful people grow up within some level of shadow – a fear that God is going to punish them somehow, somewhere, some-why. Like expecting the Roman god, Jupiter, to toss out a lightning bolt if we're late for church, or divorced, or attracted to people of the same sex. Something like that.

SHADOW: I think being gay is just one path to acquiring this fear. Faith is a different experience for all of us, so I'll just say this: for those who are living right now in Jupiter's shadow – maintaining some inner denial; holding onto a fear or guilt; waiting for God to smite you for something you have or have not done – I invite you to step away from the darkness. Seek love and self-acceptance. It's a much lighter path.

THEME: The overall theme I've aimed for is pretty simple: **know yourself.** That's it. There are lots and lots of ways to say that – like "don't let others' expectations rule your life" – or that "self awareness is the core of being fully human" – you get the idea. The bottom line for me: Be who you are. That's the best way to honor yourself, your parents, God, and everybody else on the planet.

STOMACH: Some have suggested that "Greg experiences too much through his nervous stomach." My response: In a household where dissent was discouraged and self-sacrifice was modeled, most emotions in my young life – anger, despair, desire, frustration, fear, and on.and on – expressed as stomach upset.

I didn't work to mask what young Greg felt, I offered only what he knew: his stomach hurt.

~ Gregory Gerard
August 2009

Acknowledgments

I've had so much help putting this story together. I offer sincere thanks to:

The following people for their pre-reading, suggestions, and support: Jennifer Barg, Georgia Beers, Elizabeth Boice, Kelly Cotter, Dan DeStephano, Paul Dingman, Greg DiStefano, Judy Fuller, Toby Johnson, Father Bob Kennedy, Wendy Low, Sonja Livingston, Peter Morgan, Father Bill O'Malley, Mike Potter, Julie Rivers, Kirsten Rohl, Margie Rolleston, Matt Romeiser, Caroline Sanchez-Fries, Bob Siegel, Alison Smith, Andy Tobias, Julietta Wolf-Foster, and Kate Zabel.

Michele Karlsberg, of Michele Karlsberg Marketing and Management, for her expert publicity, and all of the folks at Infinity Publishing for their top-notch quality.

All of the friends depicted in these pages; I'm forever changed for their presence in my life.

My brothers and sisters, for always making me feel cared for.

My mom, who encouraged our every dream and who recognized the healing value of fudge; my dad, who, in his aging, non-alcohol years, became the sweet family guy he always wanted to be; my gram, who was wise enough not to edit out the harshness of life when telling a story.

My partner, who's both my toughest critic and greatest strength: Jeff Denmark.

And finally, the wonderful grace of God, which makes all the rest of this matter.

BookBuilders List

Publication of this manuscript would not have been possible without the support of so many people. I'd like to highlight the names of those who made financial contributions to this project – true book builders in alpha order:

Pam Barrale and Libby Ford, Jeff Denmark, Mary Beth Kosmicki, Sonja Livingston, Gen Mancuso, Michael A. Potter, Margie Rolleston, and Sue Sweitzer.

Thank you sincerely!

About the Author

Gregory Gerard's work has been published by *Tiny Lights*, *The Stone Table Review*, and *World Voice*. He teaches writing part-time at Writers & Books, Rochester's adult literary center, and has been a guest instructor at the University of Rochester's *Scholars Creative Writing Program*. Gerard lives in Rochester, New York, with his partner of twelve years and their spitz husky.

Photo by PTM